Also by Roger King:

Love the Miracle You Are

WARRIOR LOVE

In a Changing World

ROGER KING

BALBOA.
PRESS
A DIVISION OF HAY HOUSE

Balboa Press books may be ordered through booksellers or by contacting:

Balboa Press
A Division of Hay House
1663 Liberty Drive
Bloomington, IN 47403
www.balboapress.com
1 (877) 407-4847

Because of the dynamic nature of the Internet, any web addresses or links contained in this book may have changed since publication and may no longer be valid. The views expressed in this work are solely those of the author and do not necessarily reflect the views of the publisher, and the publisher hereby disclaims any responsibility for them.

The author of this book does not dispense medical advice or prescribe the use of any technique as a form of treatment for physical, emotional, or medical problems without the advice of a physician, either directly or indirectly. The intent of the author is only to offer information of a general nature to help you in your quest for emotional and spiritual well-being. In the event you use any of the information in this book for yourself, which is your constitutional right, the author and the publisher assume no responsibility for your actions.

Any people depicted in stock imagery provided by Thinkstock are models, and such images are being used for illustrative purposes only.
Certain stock imagery © Thinkstock.

Printed in the United States of America.

ISBN: 978-1-4525-8993-0 (sc)
ISBN: 978-1-4525-8995-4 (hc)
ISBN: 978-1-4525-8994-7 (e)

Library of Congress Control Number: 2014900469

Balboa Press rev. date: 01/21/2014

This is a book that every woman could gift a man who is asking: Who am I? What lies do I need to clean up? How do I learn to love and forgive myself? So this man can give his best to life!

DEDICATIONS

Warrior love, in a rapidly changing world, is for all granddaughters, grandsons and future generations. May they know that what we do now, in learning to love who we are, helps everyone to grow in a world that is **safe** for future humans to love each other. It is dedicated to *warriors* of love like Nelson Mandela and Aung San Suu Kyi. And to all unseen warriors of love.

What we do now with our thoughts, beliefs and actions, is vital in laying foundations to create a truly loveable world. Our willingness to move from fear to love, I believe, can create a **safe** earth and a much safer, spiritual, loving and loveable race called human beings. *Warrior* love is one agreement that says: The more we each choose to love the miracle we are, the more this enhances new types of love relationships for future generations to live more peacefully and richly on planet earth.

I want this book to assist a process of growth where we can be free energetically and emotionally like a 2 to 4 year old, yet balanced like an authentically growing wise spiritual adult!

It is dedicated to Antoine De Saint–Exupery, "*The Little Prince*" in us all, where; "One must look with the heart" and become a '*warrior* of heart love', even when life throws us tough experiences!

I dedicate this book to all my families past and present and especially to my partner for the last twenty-seven years, Linda. Thank you for all your love and friendship. Thank you for being so kind and loving to my blind spots and hidden areas. You help me fly with my feet firmly on Mother Earth. Being the artistic genius you are, may you know in your heart that our lives are growing with the *big* love we have shared. Let us live with wonderful memories and without regret or shame. Be all that you are!

To Jessica, Shelley, and Simon, my three children whom I love: thank you for all the love and nourishment you have given me. When people talk to me about you, they genuinely tell me what inspiring and strong souls you are.

I also dedicate this book to all my teachers, famous and not famous, and to all the people who have visited me in my counseling garden hut and have had faith in me and have shared their stories. I dedicate this work to friends who have shared their hearts and helped me see life with such gratitude, joy, and courage. As I dance on the warm veranda under a half moon on the island of Crete, I think of all who have attended my Heal Your Life workshops. Thank you. Your inspiration for learning to love yourselves has assisted me in my awareness, consciousness, and transformation. Thank you for the fun and laughs and the tears we shared as we unfolded our secret lives.

I give sincere gratitude to Chelle Thompson (www.inspirationline.com) for her willingness to edit my early manuscripts and for loving me through my fear of publishing this book.

Thank you, Louise Hay. If I could take only one audio CD to my Greek island, Crete, it would be *You Can Heal Your Life*. To me one ingredient for success is listening daily to inspiring positive information, especially when life is giving you apparent setbacks.

I thank the divine mind that prompted me to attract Konstantina and her beautiful mountain villa. May we always be friends. I had affirmed daily: "The right place to stay is on the checkerboard of life in Crete." And here it is!

I want to thank my soul sister, who has listened to and shared so many of my stories. She has believed in me, especially when I doubted myself. And I thank all my friends—you know who you are!

I send a spirit message of love to my father and mother, whom I chose, and who, I now believe, chose me. I hope I have learned or am learning the lessons I was sent here to learn! You were the perfect parents even in the gift of imperfection.

A big heartfelt thank you to my website manager, Richard Gentle, who is an amazingly soft and loveable man and talented spiritual writer: www.richardgentle.co.uk. He is a star in my life.

Heartfelt thanks to a genius John Welding for his childlike illustrations: www.johnwelding.comix.org.uk

Thank you Balboa Press. The process started with Joey urging me to publish and then Janelle, Brandon, Rebecca and Jan for having enormous patience. My heart goes out to you all.

As I write this preface and dedication, I play, with the volume up and tears coming, a Jimmy Cliff version of the song, "I Can See Clearly Now" by Johnny Nash.

> *I can see clearly now the rain is gone,*
> *I can see all obstacles in my way.*
> *Gone are the dark clouds that had me blind*
> *It's gonna be a bright, bright, sun-shiny day.*

And so it is.

I also dedicate this inner journey to the creative healing power I have received from all the great musicians and singers I play in my work as a "Dancing DJ." Composers and singers like Bob Marley and John Lennon, who learned a kind of *warrior* love that has inspired so many young and old with their dream of love for this world.

The reason I have used stories from major spiritual traditions is that I love to think the masters gave their teachings in parables and stories. And I love to hear stories myself and tell them. I thank Bill Darlison, author and minister emeritus of the Dublin Unitarian Church, for his permission to use short stories from his book, *The Shortest Distance*. He is a lovely soul who is a fountain of gentle wisdom.

I would like to add, that every attempt was made to credit all sources whenever applicable. Anyone with additional information is encouraged to contact: Permissions Department Balboa press. Any errors will be corrected on future reprints.

Lastly, I thank you, the reader, for reading this book. I truly believe you are on your way to finding an infinite well of love, joy, peace, and wisdom within you. Your increasing honesty will help create love not fear!

Every effort has been made to locate copyright holders of the stories used in this book. Please contact me if I have inadvertently infringed any copyright and I will gladly remedy this in any future edition.

THE POWER OF RETREAT

I want to invite all who read this book to go on a retreat with me into the desert of your lives, where possible negative secrets you have bought into, whether consciously or unconsciously, throughout your short or long life, come to the surface. A retreat is a place where you can take yourself out of the daily life of job (or no job), listening to news, watching TV, reading newspapers, playing on computers, and dealing with people. Here, you live with your evolving truth. All the great teachers went into the desert to re-find the truth of what they believed beyond all conditioning. Your retreat to find your truth maybe to meditate, go for a walk. It might be in your kitchen, your bedroom, the little room, the bath, or a garden hut. I have often retreated to my own counseling hut. You could be in a mental prison or an actual institution of despair. I ask you: "Can you find your retreat, somewhere safe to learn and be conscious of being the real you, and then embrace changes you see in the mirror of your life?"

I call you to share my retreat in the mountains of Crete! It is a kind of desert where there is a wonderful oasis that calls you inside to uncover who you truly are: a spiritual being having a temporary physical experience called life! I realize this may seem like a strange request, yet it is a most profound journey to be alone in a mountain desert where only the sun, moon, and stars are listening to the "inner chatterbox" that slows your life right down. This is a rebirthing retreat in which we may receive guidance for mind, body and soul.

"*Warrior* Love"

What would a world be like with *warrior* love?

I had a dream that all humans are 'dissolving' negative beliefs. These beliefs stop us from learning to love and heal our hearts from rejection and hurt of all kinds.

Warrior love is about creating a climate within our mind, body, and soul, where it is safer for us to love each other – by starting with our self as a true miracle of life that can choose to shine faith with honest self-love rather than fear. You may think this is utopian and I am crazy! However, if we carry on as we are, living in fear of intimacy and love, I believe our grandchildren and their children will grow up with increasing fear and anxiety and an earth reflecting this mindset could say: "*your time is up!*"

I want to join with humanity on learning how to be brave with *warrior* love, how we can reconnect to life with authentic 'heart love', in communion with spiritual growth and sexual honesty. *Warrior* love is about that deep search inside ourselves for a love that we did not experience with parents who often did not know how to love who they were.

Warrior love holds no blame, no judgment, and no fear. It loves like a tree, a flower, a river flowing. *Warrior* love feels like talking and listening to the divine pulse in everything. *Warrior* love is experiencing love in every breath, thought and feeling. *Warrior* love opens your heart to living in the power of *now*.

I believe we are constantly changing and are capable of loving more than one person at the same time. I suggest *warrior* love is learning to be *honest* about our need to relate to different people emotionally and possibly sexually. However, we need to learn how to truly cope with the emotions and gut-wrenching feelings of jealousy, lies and hypocrisy that our conditioning can manifest in us. If we completely deny our capacity for *warrior* love, this can hide us in marriages that gradually feel less and less loving and creative.

The quiet revolution of abundant warrior love

I suggest *warrior* love is about exploring our capacity to draw from an infinite wise well of love. That loving relationships are the norm and we are naturally good at loving, where we no longer allow our parasitical negative conditioning to puncture our natural ability to be love, loving and loveable.

I suggest that we need alternative ways of reconnecting to *warrior* love. I believe we need different people at different times in our life that bring fresh love into our lives; that one partner for life, often cannot suffice for our real needs. Our conditioned fear so often says, "*no!* I want just one person to love me and nobody else." Where the fear of abandonment is too much.

I suggest we need new relationship choices and the one I talk about later in this book is Polyamory – which simply means we openly and honestly love more than one person and are learning without guilt or shame to be honest to our primary partner and vice-versa.

I believe we can learn how to reduce jealousy and making each other and ourselves wrong for this *open* relationship change! Monogamy has served us as one model for many generations. However, people are becoming increasingly separated, because we, as individuals, are rapidly changing and one reason for this is that we are learning to love who we truly are. This in turn can make us more loving and loveable. This new way of being needs to be embraced and understood otherwise future children will grow up in an atmosphere of conflict and arguments of "who is right?" and "who is wrong?"

A new consciousness creates a new reality

With self-help books and therapies, we learn about our different energies of self-love, self-compassion and self-worth. These qualities are gradually permeating into consciousness. However, often it is only one person in a partnership that is willing to grow, and the partner who is working on their past hurt becomes frustrated on many levels and can choose to seek love elsewhere. (I realize this is a generalization).

So this dream and vision is to challenge us as humans that we are born to love and be love. That if we increase (authentic) teachings of self-love we need to create a conscious society and culture that validates more honesty about our need to seek "open love" that learns to dissolve jealousy, lies and abuse. I believe we can do it with powerful inner wisdom.

In my opinion, I wonder if mankind was helped to be more aware and conscious about our ability to love more than one person, and we chose to be free to love with openness and honesty, could wars stop and slavery in all its forms cease? Could spiritual and sexual abuse and negative addictions of all kinds dissolve by learning what I call *warrior* love? We need to be brave with inner wisdom and create strong role models that can wake us up to our abiltiy to love without shame, guilt and fear.

Warrior love is about creating a culture where it is safe to be open and honest about our ability to love openly—not hiding and hurting others and losing integrity. I ask: "Can we shift in consciousness about our (apparently hard-wired) jealous feelings if our partner is attracted to someone else?" What would our society be like if each of us took our personal power to share more openly, communicating honestly about our emotional and sexual needs, without vilification? Nearly everyone learns, in our monogamous society, that spouses have exclusive rights to each other. We are conditioned to feel that if our partner is interested in someone else we will be replaced—or that it is a personal rejection of ourselves.

Imagine a culture where your partner's attraction to another created increased pleasure, joy and intimacy for you. Would jealousy be such a monumental experience of destruction? So *warrior* love asks each of us to look at the questions: How does jealousy affect me? And what can I do about it? Must I feel ashamed for having jealous thoughts? Could I learn with openness and deep sharing, not to let those feelings swamp me? A news report informed us that there is an increased awareness of sex at much younger ages, and one concerning consequence of this is increasing non-consensual sex (rape)—especially around the poorer estates in cities. With [often young] men, being in a confused *mind set* to grab intimacy through rape, this is such a signal that there is never a better time, I suggest, for learning "warrior love"—where we teach and mentor positive ways to love our self and then love each other. We no longer blame anyone, especially our parents, partners, or ourselves. We dissolve our parasite of negative domestication. We become aware with active consciousness to transform our lives through fewer lies with open living. We learn to manage trauma, intensity, and unequal sex drives, with less jealousy and addictions. The judge and the victim no longer control our mind. Our minds become fertile for intense and active love and a new dream is born. We are energy and as we increase consciousness we can use this force for good—not abuse and enslavement towards women and children. And men become free of being the abuser or wrongdoer.

How?

Children love to be loved by adults who love themselves from a place of deep personal integrity.

Imagine that our children are mentored in strong self-esteem, *warrior love,* from year one, by parents and teachers who love who they are; experiencing self-love, especially at school and other places of learning. This would be such an exciting adventure for young minds. Children love to be listened to about all subjects, especially learning to love self without shame and guilt. I believe bullying and early abuse dissolves together with wise boundaries of self-love and self-knowledge. I see warrior love being taught in schools and through college life and even in businesses and government organizations. Warrior love includes teachings that serve our rich humanity—not just cramming knowledge.

In my vision, men and women of all generations dissolve their "secret lives" that come from stories of pain, and alchemize them with becoming "brave" with truth. We learn Toltec wisdom from teachers like Don Miquel Ruiz:

To be impeccable with our word; where we no longer take things personally; we no longer make assumptions; and we always do our best.

Our healing energies increase moment by moment as we create new beliefs and agreements that assist right-action to heal the "dream" of this wounded earth. We create a culture that mentors and shares what helps to create loving relationships with self and others. This information, with practice and will power, becomes a priority for each of us to learn. Enlightened women, men, and children become our authentic *warrior* guides and we learn to trust each other through trusting our inner power of *warrior* love.

Forgiveness and letting go blame, by men and women, becomes our hallmark of regaining trust. No longer do we stay victims with a harsh judge. We become *dream masters*. We become truly responsible by being intuitively wild and free. Self-love opens us to a key that opens our heart; our story is shared with "brave vulnerable truth." We choose to love and become *warrior* love – even when life is tough.

Money becomes a transaction of abundant love. There is only one world – no third world! Feminine energy is wisely integrated into business and all transactions. Co-operation of skill and knowledge opens new avenues of sustainable methods of living.

Religions no longer compete for our minds. Each soul is a priestess or priest. Life is seen and experienced as an exciting school that unfolds with delightful surprises. People's minds, bodies, and souls, wake up from being negatively domesticated. When we become aware that we are not free, we take right action to be truly free from a virus of self-destruction. Chaos becomes a true heaven on earth.

Families, communities and countries co-operate. Manipulation through guilt, resentment, criticism, jealousy and fear are dissolved by being constantly connected to the power of spiritual and sexual healing energies within each of us. We learn to wake every day with gratitude and practice *the gentle art of blessing*. As we build gratitude we attract prosperity of every kind: Friends, time, good health, and wisdom.

Instead of being victims, *warrior* love assists people inside work organizations to free their hearts and attract work they love. Humans share with a *warrior* heart to become brave and truthful with all that they think, say, and do.

As we embrace *warrior* love we create a paradigm shift of consciousness to live an enlightened life that creates miracles of healing whenever needed. We no longer survive; we live our love energy in the *now*.

Change is healthy, as we become open and receptive to being truthful to our partners and ourselves. "Time to think" with friendly thoughts and beliefs in our minds is natural. People listen to themselves and each other with love, forgiveness, and appreciation. We make real advances in being truthful about our spiritual and sexual desires. Our "earth guide only" (ego) is loved in such a way that it moves us from fear to authentic love. We don't fight our ego, we dissolve its fear around our death. Because we realize we never die, we just transmute into spirit of a higher vibration of love.

Governments and religious leaders of countries are made up of people who love life and new agreements are made with consciousness and easily kept. Ageing reverses, worry is dissolved, and we realize we could live for an average of 200 years and move onto the next training ground with ease. Our words, thoughts and actions are creative when connected with meditation, prayer and disciplined *warrior* action. We speak and sing a new language of heartfelt affirmations. This gives the Source clear and wise messages that we are "ready" to be totally connected to the power of being at *one* with Source.

Humans choose to dissolve the parasite of fear that comes from the negative mass media and many other sources. Our whole drama of false beliefs and negative agreements are seen and transformed through actions of intense *warrior* love. Our impeccable word "hovers over the water" and we give thanks from our infinite heart of love and healthy love returns multiplied. And so it is.

Reflect

Just close your eyes, and then open your inner eye and see love coming from the heart of every star, from the heart of every tree, from the heart of every rock, from every pulsating heart of every human being. No longer do you live with the virus of fear of what others think. You no longer judge harshly. You no longer fear being rejected. You no longer feel emotionally or sexually abnormal. You are not afraid to lose anything—including your life. You no longer live with beliefs based on lies or misinformation.

You wake up! Imagine if this dream and vision was true and our thoughts, feelings, words and actions learned to create this dream through awareness, consciousness and transformation. This inner journey is asking us all to become *"warrior* love" creating an ever-expanding mind that opens our heart.

Warrior love asks: Why do animals punish only once, while we humans can punish others and ourselves thousands of times with our thoughts and feelings? Could we learn to forgive quickly or do we seek vengeance? Does this bring real justice and a safer world for our children's children?

"Wake up Roger!" My old teacher said to me. "Stop feeling sorry for yourself and live now!" What I believe is we really wake up when we realize love is who we are and we feel its presence in ourselves and everywhere at the same moment of time.

What I believe

Men and women can make a choice to love self with knowledge, skill and a willpower that does not deny the present chaos we have created on earth. I want to assist us to choose love and life! By choosing love we can come home to earth and dissolve our lies and secrets. Women; I ask you not to *beat* us [men] with your hurt anger. That will only help to hurt this earth and create more chaos on earth. I believe men do want to positively change and grow and dissolve the lies we hold. However, we need to be positively and creatively mentored. I believe boys, teenagers and men are yearning to know how to love their true capacity for *safe* and authentic love.

As my tears flow with sadness and laughter at how funny we all are, my message is simple, though maybe not easy—I ask you to embrace: *Warrior* Love in an ever changing and challenging world.

This is one man's inner journey, asking questions, and seeking possible answers, that our human consciousness may find unusual and challenging, with the intention of disarming conflict with empathy, truth, love, music, dance, and stories.

Roger King
August 2013
Paleochora, Crete

INTRODUCTION

My invitation is to journey to the "power within"—a *warrior* power that calls us to embody qualities of listening to and learning about courage, love, joy, peace, forgiveness, and wisdom. This book is about one man's search for openness and honesty ... about replacing fear with love consciousness.

I would like you to take these thoughts into the book you are about to read. I suggest you return to them as you read the book.

Louise Hay: *"When I experience a problem, and we all have them, I immediately say: "Out of this situation, only good will come. This is easily resolved for the highest good of all concerned. All is well and I am safe."*

Sondra Ray: *"One definition of love is ultimate self-approval. If you love yourself, you will automatically give others the opportunity to love you."*

Deborah Anapol: *"Love is inherently free. It cannot be bought, sold, or traded."*

Or as Paulo Coelho puts it, *"In love lies the seed of our growth. The more we love, the closer we are to the spiritual experience."*

David Deida: "Giving Love—to the point of recognizing existence as love—is the purpose of your life.

Don Miquel Ruiz: *"Become impeccable with your word. Don't take things personally, don't make assumptions and always do your best ... And know each time you break these agreements you can start again."*

Robert Holden adds, *"Love is about everything ... When you make love your purpose, you are fulfilling your destiny."*

Fred Lehrman states, *"The Immortal Relationship will be real for you to the extent that you can let go of two fundamental lies about your existence which you may have accepted at your birth: first, that love comes from outside of you; second, that you need love to survive. What is true is this: You are love, and nothing can kill you."*

Brene Brown: *"I now see how owning our story and loving ourselves through that process is the bravest thing that we will ever do."*

Masaru Emoto: *"Water secretly holds two energies: one of love and one of gratitude."*

Let me begin the story by inviting the inspiration: Patañjali was the author of Yoga Sutras. He lived around the second century BC. He wrote, *"When you are inspired ... dormant forces, faculties and talents become alive, and you discover yourself to be a greater person by far than you ever dreamed yourself to be."*

Life goes in cycles. I am in a process of parting from someone I have loved. Somewhere I still love her; however, we have both changed. This book tells my story and about my loving myself during a particularly "tough" transition. There is a time to experience my truth, and then let go and move on. When I don't listen to that voice of spirit and see inside and outside what is happening in life, I let life get difficult. I start to lie to others and myself. I can begin to blame, which makes my life stuck. This makes me imagine what's wrong with me and everybody else! I fear telling the truth because I may hurt someone I love, or I run scared because the present brings up pain from the past. This has a negative effect on every *hado*—a Japanese word for subtle vibration—in my cellular body. Resentment from old anger can lead me to kill my body and leave earth before I have learned my lessons of unconditional love. So let's move on.

In his audio, *Touching the Earth: Guided Meditations for Mindfulness Practice*, Vietnamese Zen Buddhist monk Thích Nhất Hạnh said: *"I am not bound to the idea of permanence… When we bow down we have to be prepared to let go. We have to surrender our resentment."*

It is important to listen when life sends you a message repeatedly to let go of a loving partner of nearly twenty-seven years duration. This book is a process of learning lessons from my actions and choices that have hurt two lovely souls and our grown-up children. I want to repent from my heart for certain choices. I want to become enlightened and heal. I want to handle relationships, as spiritual lessons. Sondra Ray puts it this way: *"A partner will bring up all your patterns. Don't avoid relationships; they are the best seminar in town. The truth is that your partner is your guru. Because they help you get healed."* Later she adds: *"So don't resent them when you get into upsets."*

On the power of intention Gandhi wrote: *"My life is my message."*

I want this book to accord my partner and me the dignity our spiritual and sexual union deserves. I want it to give authentic love and respect to our family members, friends, and anyone who knows us. I risk rejection and judgment as I unfold my story. Yet my life is my message to men and women to help them own their stories. I also intend for it to be a book for people who have survived abusive families, so we can stand up for ourselves and stop feeling and believing that we are unlovable. I want us all to become courageously positive and authentically take our true power! I call it *warrior* love.

I intend for this book to be about expanding our awareness and consciousness to the following questions: How can men be attracted to loving themselves with a willingness to dissolve the lies that we so often believe about ourselves? Can men, on a huge scale, love becoming honest and authentic? Can we live with women and know we are *radically* honest about learning to love the "miracle power" inside us? Is it possible for men to trust other men? Can we dissolve the need to be so jealous? Can we learn to balance our masculine and feminine energies? Can men *come out* and be true with deep sensitivity? Can we give to this earth our best love and give up greed? Are we willing to live our lives radically differently and positively, and become part of the solution rather than another part of a growing problem?

I suggest reading this book from beginning to end. If you take it in bits only, you risk judging harshly and losing the lessons. So often our words are taken out of context because our own hurt leaps upon those words. After you read the book, just open it where your mind and spirit direct, and it may just speak to you! Do write me and give your *warrior* love feedback—even if it's tough love! I am always open to learning more each day from real souls who are willing to love themselves.

My life's purpose

I am a man whose life is dedicated to assisting myself and other people to know it's okay to love yourself—especially when life is tough.

Throughout forty years of work, I have been privileged to witness a climate of new beliefs being sown in the garden of people's minds and an incredible ability to find an inner power to change their lives against all odds for the better. Simply, I teach humans (by being a willing conduit myself) to love themselves by replacing beliefs that are based on lies. I teach them to sow the belief that they *can* freely choose to support a new life of love, truth, creativity, and peace. I am constantly learning from each person I work with, so I am continually working on my dark corners, as you will read in this book.

My calling

I invite you to come to a place where all the questions you've ever asked yourself are answered from deep inside the emerging authentic you.

I journey to the power within. I believe this wise, all-knowing power can help us dissolve lies we have heard and believed about ourselves and about how life needs to be lived just to fit in to a so-called norm. Everyday reality can dictate our reactions to life, and the "to do" lists become seemingly endless. Whereas a retreat to the desert enables each of us to see more clearly, open the heart of our mind, and reveal the fundamental truth that we are vast miracles of love in the making.

I feel truly challenged to rise above all limitations and go through a healing process of change. I invite you to join me. Hopefully, you will come through the journey with some insights about your ability to find love deep inside you and heal what has stopped you from being connected to this whole-hearted you. This is a book for men, but also for women—both adults and teenagers. Yet I am so aware that we men can feel so alone and often protect ourselves with appearing okay, yet crying out for love inside. I want to serve men by saying it's truly okay to love *you*; to let you know you can change your life by learning love as an *inside job*! I want to share the possibility that male energy can be truly self-healing.

As I relay my story, I ask one favor: Will you please suspend your judgments? Watch those critical thoughts; you may learn something about yourself, your beliefs, and your possible prejudices inside your subconscious mind. You may fear what I may say about myself. Well, I ask you to go beyond your surface reaction and dive deeper.

Learning about love and how to love

If you have ever been in a relationship with another person that has gone past its time, then you may have some empathy for this inner journey. If you have ever asked questions like: Who am I? What is my purpose? What is Love? Then this retreat may be life-changing for you. I welcome you and your entire story… your beliefs, race, religion, sexual preferences, prejudices, fears, criticisms, guilt, and deep resentment at the lies you have allowed to *condition* you. Often I experience people cry for "what could have been" as they let love heal their past and present lives. Don't wait any longer *do it now*. Don't wait for everything to be right; you might be on your deathbed by then!

I want to know who I am, and I want to connect to you in that oasis of truth that goes beyond our personalities and the masks we put on to survive. I will use stories to go past our hurt and pain to discover what wise and truly unconditional loving spirits you and I are.

As a counselor for many years, I have listened to many people say, "If only I wasn't married anymore, I would be happy!" Or, "If only he (or she) were different then …" Or, "What would people say if I left the relationship (job, church, synagogue, or mosque)?" Or, "I wish I could meet the right person; then I would be happy." Or, "I wish I had more money; then I would…" Or, "I wish I wasn't brought up a Catholic (Jew or Protestant or Muslim)." Or, "What if my church (my friends, my co-workers, my family) knew what I was really like!" And sometimes, "I wish I had never been born!"

What I want to hear from those who read this book is this: "Thank God somebody heard me. Someone knows what it's like to be me!" I want to know what lies you have chosen to hold onto because of fear in order to create your own so-called "real world" of toughness, isolation and *dis-ease*. I want to facilitate our healing through sharing our vulnerable selves with a *heart,* breaking open with truth. This creates, I believe, an open heart… vast, passionate, and vulnerable… that can realign us to our true selves and convey infinitely more love than we have experienced before. I want you to consider love as a way of being independent of any other person. That love is a state of consciousness. As clinical psychologist Dr. Deborah Anapol says about love that she learned from her teachers: *"The thing is, love is a choice you can only make for yourself, not for anyone else."* Instead of " falling in love" helplessly or accidentally, they [her teachers]… spoke of "rising in love" after removing all resistance. When we love ourselves without resistance, then I believe we become a *warrior* of love! Judgment and taking offense are outside the space of love. I realize now love is an infinite space where we can dissolve fear and all our negative conditioning, especially our fear of self.

The power of fear

My first story is aimed at all those who worry that people might find out who they really are—especially those who would literally think and feel suicidal thoughts if people found out. Even death for some hurt souls seems to be a better place than being truthful and dissolving those bullying thoughts and feelings!

The Snake in the Cup

One day a businessman was drinking a cup of tea at the house of a female business acquaintance when he noticed what he thought was a baby snake in his cup. Not wishing to embarrass his hostess, he gulped down the tea—snake and all—and hastily left.

The thought of the tiny snake in his stomach really distressed the man. For the rest of the day he felt nauseated, and when he went to bed that night he had terrible stomach ache. Fearing that he may have contracted some terrible disease from the snake, or worse, that the snake was still alive and was gnawing his insides, he resolved to visit the doctor as soon as possible. Early in the morning, after a very disturbed night's sleep, he set out for the doctor's surgery.

On the way he passed the house where he had swallowed the snake. His friend, who happened to be looking out of the window, noticed his miserable condition and invited him inside. The sick man sat where he had sat before, and politely accepted another cup of tea, but as he raised the cup to drink, he saw another snake! He threw the cup to the floor and quickly explained his impolite behavior to his puzzled friend. She smiled and pointed to the ceiling, where a short length of rope was dangling. "There's your snake," said his friend. "What you thought was a baby snake was a reflection of a little piece of rope!" The man's stomach pain disappeared immediately, and he was back to perfect health in an hour.

Who, as a child, feared that the coat hanging behind the door was a burglar? And as the book of Proverbs suggests: *"For as he thinketh in his heart, so is he."* (Proverbs 23:7, King James Version). Often we let our imagination create those ghosts, and we stay in fear. So what snakes do you imagine you may have swallowed into your subconscious mind, which still make you uncomfortable or even distressed? Now let's begin a journey together as equals in mind, body, and spirit.

Arrival in Crete

I bless my partner with love as she dives deep into her pain of parting from me and regains her self-worth and self-compassion.

I have reached the age of sixty-five and my gift to myself is one month in a mountain retreat near a lovely town called Paleochora in southern Crete.

I am sitting in the bus station in the heat of the bustling city of Chania (it's 37 degrees Celsius, 98.6 degrees Fahrenheit) waiting for my smart green Mercedes coach to take me onward. Strangled Greek music and rich oily food smells drift across my senses. Organized chaos is brimming over in the heat. I feel my heart pound with excitement and joy of being back in a safe place, *Crete!*

Being safe

To feel safe is such a human need, especially when we delve into the loving and exacting power within, where truth uncovers a process that makes us feel vulnerable … where tears flow and anger erupts, yet we still know we are held in loving arms of grace and deep consciousness. It is where "being" all parts of who we are meets consciousness and transformation begins.

This book is an inner journey, and I invite you to join me. It is a perfect time to be here in Crete. I feel I am going out on a limb, risking deep changes in my life path—"the shift" as motivational speaker, Wayne Dyer, calls it, "from ambition to meaning." It is a journey to the afternoon and evening of a meaningful life!

Dive deep with me!

So as I dive daily into the warm blue Libyan sea, I ask you to dive in too. The message in this book is divided into a series of dives (some quite beautifully fierce) inside to the "power within"! I know I need divine inspiration, which I ask for daily, and moment-by-moment in my meditations and affirmation prayers. Let me tell you a story about those hidden gifts we all have when we take risks to go into a desert retreat.

I affirm you may find this book similar to the story from poet, philosopher, and scholar John O'Donohue in his book *Anam Cara: A Book of Celtic Wisdom*.

The king and the beggar's gift

Once upon a time there lived a king who was so popular that his subjects would often bring him gifts just to show him how much they loved him. They brought him exquisite ornaments, expensive jewelry, fashionable clothing, exotic foods and spices. The king received these graciously, and felt very humbled by the generosity of his subjects. One day, a shabbily dressed man appeared at the palace. "I would like to see the king," he told the palace guard. "I have a special gift for him."

The king wasn't terribly busy that day and so the poor man was shown into his presence. He bowed low before his sovereign, and taking out a melon from his bag, he said: "Your majesty, please accept this melon as a token of my esteem and affection." The king thanked him politely, but since he didn't much like melons, he handed it to a servant and told him to throw it into the back yard.

The next week the poor man appeared again, and once more he presented the king with a melon. As before, the king told the servant to throw it away. This went on week after week, but the king was too polite to tell the man that he wasn't eating the melons.

One day, just as the man was about to hand over the melon, the king's pet monkey jumped down from the window ledge where it had been sitting and knocked the melon to the ground smashing it to pieces. When the king looked at the mess on the floor he noticed on the floor a glistening stone. He picked it up and found that it was a diamond; a bigger diamond than any he had ever seen in his life. He immediately went to the back yard of the palace where the other melons had been thrown, and, sure enough, in the middle of all the rotting fruit, there were numerous huge diamonds.

What I want to emphasize with this book and my story is the spiritual principle that the things we don't like often can contain the greatest treasures. Sharing our negative beliefs, our tears, our lies, our angers, and our guilt can invite the Source to heal the wounds we bear from these experiences. With one proviso, we don't become a victim to that pain. And you might ask yourself, when in your life have things you thought were going to be awful, become a source of healing, inspiration and happiness? I know I have made many mistakes by holding onto lies about life and myself. Yet I know divine love holds me through those dark nights of soul retrieval.

DIVE

1

Choices

My waking thought: *It is safe for me to grow, even when life requires tough choices.*

Let me ask you, the reader: Who would be fearful, critical, or jealous of you if you changed by loving yourself, and then shining that love and the powerful miracle within you, to create a whole new way of being and living? One consequence of your changing could be attracting new intimate relationships into your life, new ways of being creative, new ways of living with the earth. A whole new vista of life could open up.

Who would *not* want you to change and grow into a powerful person in your own right? Would it be your partner, your children, or people who think they know you?

Raising awareness and consciousness through therapy or self-help groups or books, or teachers who cross your path may bring the realization that your life needs to change. Often self-made confusion through feeling fear can mask the true change that is happening. Lots of inner excuses tell us not to change: "don't rock the boat." There is one part in us—the "old us"—that wants everything to stay the same. However, our deeper desire is to become true to the person that is deeply buried under this fear. There is, I believe, a time to rebirth the miracle we were born with. This can happen when we nearly die or experience a crisis or catastrophe such as a partner leaving. I think we re-connect consciously with the heart energy of love. We can call this power Divine

1

Mind, Universal Mind, God, Goddess, or Higher Self. We do come back to our spiritual home of being truly spirit having a temporary human physical body.

Deep change

This deeper change I now face. I have come to encounter, digest, and assimilate the challenge of my second wife and I going our separate ways and doing this with as much kindness, wisdom, love, forgiveness, and truth as we can. I love her, yet our ways of seeing and experiencing love and reality are not compatible.

In my first marriage, I found it so hard to believe I could change and grow. I am not blaming my partner. I was frightened of what others might say. I left after twelve years of not being myself. You see, I never knew who I was. I just reacted to survive. I did the best I knew how with the awareness I had then. Fear paralyzed me to the point that I blamed parents, sisters, schools, church, and most of all myself!

As my arrested inner child dictated, all I knew was, *I must never tell the truth. People will hurt me and make me feel stupid.* The man I was then was confused, had no real self-knowledge, and was filled with such hurt. I was on the "inner telephone," as one of my teachers put it, so I never really listened or learned how to live with authentic, responsible, personal power. My chatterbox was full of self-doubt.

Sound familiar to you? I thought, *everybody else must change before I can be free to make new choices.* I became the classic victim, and of course, my main thought was: *There is no money to be free!*

I thought of all the reasons why I could not change. The word *can't* was in the forefront of my mind. Now *can* remains after removing the apostrophe and the *t.* I had no faith or trust that anything "out there" or within me existed that would assist me in making a positive change. I became a taker, a victim, and my own worst judge. I bored everyone with my hard-luck story and felt sorry for myself.

Being responsible with compassion and self-compassion

This book is written in contrition, not shame. I know I am not a bad man. I take full responsibility for the poor choices I made in the latter years of our marriage.

I realize I have taken from those I love by keeping secrets and by lying about my need for an intimacy that my partner could not give me. I believe she has changed, and now I cannot give her what she truly needs. The person I have become is not perfect, and, thank you, reader, I hope you are not. Perfectionism is a killer; it hides who we are. That's not an excuse. I risk feeling shame at present, and I wake in the middle of the night feeling desolate and imagining people gossiping about my choices and behaviors. Yet I am learning to have what research professor Dr. Brené Brown calls, "self-compassion" to "develop shame resilience." Not listening and recognizing the need for change can be so painful if, like me, you have learned to lie for fear of losing love or because you feel unlovable.

Wanting others to change rather than changing yourself

One truth I realize I wanted my partner to change to how I wanted her to be. I felt I would be happy then. But I cannot change anyone, only myself. I know this in theory, yet I denied my power and responsibility to come out and say, "I am changing. It's time to be honest about who I am and what I need."

One big lesson I learned is that, when I choose to stay silent and not say what I need in a relationship, I hurt my partner as well as myself. I know now I cannot earn anyone's approval by hiding behind the deception of getting my needs met elsewhere. And I am not going to beat myself up for changing as a human being.

However, I could have listened to my inner power, which so often prompted me to be truthful. But I was too afraid of the consequences. I thought that by being honest, I would hurt those I loved. This circular thinking deepened my confusion. So, reader, listen carefully to what is changing within you. Remember that the longer you delay being honest, the more hurt will come to you. So many of us—men especially—isolate ourselves, pretending to be okay while running scared inside. We compartmentalize our secret lives. Eventually these secrets unfold, often prompted by crisis, and then we are encouraged to be truthful in every area of life, past and present. Well, my partner choosing to leave me is my prompt.

The fear of lack and not deserving

While I was growing up, I never felt there was enough money, and this linked indelibly in my consciousness to the lack of love in my original family. As a result, I gave up my power to earn my own money when I married and, most importantly, my ability to charge a fair price for doing what I was clever at, which was working with people as a therapist, counselor, and group leader. I loved my work and did it with as much patience and love as I could muster. Yet I felt somewhere I was not worthy.

This became a large area of resentment for me and for my partner. I relied on another person, my wife's kind father, to provide financially for my family and me. This does not bring self-respect.

Taking back my power

I truly want to take responsibility with heartfelt forgiveness and love for what has happened. An old proverb says, "You get what you think about whether you want it or not." So I watch carefully what I think and say. And moreover, I watch what I put into my mind daily. What do you think and say about your life moment-to-moment, day in day out? Are you critical with your mind to your wonderful body? Well, read this story:

The Stag at the Pool

A thirsty stag went to get a drink from a pool. Having satisfied his thirst, he lingered for a moment, looking at his reflection in the water. What fine antlers I have, he thought. They spread out so wide and look so strong that I'm sure all the other creatures envy me. Then he noticed how thin and weak his legs looked. If only my legs were as impressive as my antlers, I'd be a very beautiful beast indeed!

As he was thinking these things, a lion spotted him and began to give chase. The stag took off and easily outpaced the lion in the clearing, but as soon as the stag entered a wood, his antlers caught in the branches of some trees. Try as he might, he couldn't disentangle himself. In fact, the more he struggled, the more trapped he became. Soon the lion caught up with him and attacked him. With his dying breath the stag said, "Oh how mistaken I was! I despised my legs which were keeping me from death, and I boasted about my antlers which have been my ruin."

Insight: Sometimes we could benefit from choosing to value what we value least. What aspects of life do we take for granted—despise even—yet would cause us to feel impoverished if we were denied them? Perhaps it is finding love within ourselves and then realizing we are truly lovable. As *A Course in Miracles* puts it succinctly: *"Identify with love, and you are safe. Identify with love, and you are home. Identify with love and find yourself.*

A secret: We become what we think about! So I choose *warrior* love and one aspect of *warrior* love is self-compassion.

Self-Compassion assists the inner journey

The twenty-minute "TEDx" talk is so clear on the well-researched benefits of practicing a self-compassion, called "The Space Between Self-Esteem and Self Compassion" by Dr Kristin Neff.

This short YouTube video is learning the difference between self-esteem and self-compassion.

Do you give yourself self-compassion? The three elements are: "Self-Kindness, Common Humanity, and Mindfulness". I am always intrigued by how to do things, the "why?" often I see comes later. So how does self-compassion help me build *warrior* love?

I want to relate to myself with self-kindness, especially going through this parting of two searching souls. Writing this book is being kind and warm to myself, it's not just being critical of me! With self-compassion, I can integrate the thoughts and feelings that what is happening is very human. I do know in my heart that my sufferings are a common experience throughout humanity and so it's not just happening to *me* alone! I don't have to hide and just go into feeling a "bad" person! I can go out and connect to others. Next, I want to learn "Mindfulness." This is taking a balanced approach to my feelings; neither to exaggerate nor deny my negative emotions of self-criticism.

The critical belief of *"I must not be lazy"*

If I beat myself up continually, I just leave the planet early without learning unconditional love. I can get lost in my own pain. I want to consciously learn to be kind to me. When I criticize myself I am threatening and attacking myself. I become the threat and the threatened. The fight-flight response kicks in. My stress response shuts my immune system down and I can become ill and depressed. The old negative belief that I need to be self-critical comes from a protestant belief: work hard and harder—so I won't be lazy. This can lead to exhaustion! So I affirm:

"I wisely build self-compassion by meditating regularly which helps me learn and be open and receptive to learning the next step for personal growth."

I choose love even when life is tough so self-compassion can give the deep genuine experience to feel safe. I begin to think what I truly need from the heart of my mind. I need to tap into warmth and soft vocalizations of genuine positive affirmations. When I feel safe I choose to meditate and respond with wisdom and compassion for others who are close to me, yet knowing I need self-compassion. So I repeatedly choose to tap into nurturing myself. I do yoga and juice with good organic ingredients. I eat regularly and keep fit, watch a funny film. I put on my rich soul music (as you will see throughout this book) dance wild or soft and let grief flow. I send gentle blessings of love to all who maybe critical of me at this time. I see and think clearly and let self-compassion facilitate positive change. I write my story with self-compassion. One beautiful way of attracting self-compassion is to choose carefully whom I share my pain with. Today the right person came to listen and just let me cry.

Some of the ingredients for choosing love, especially when life is tough, and so learning Warrior Love, are the following:

- To be willing to learn the lessons from what I have attracted.
- To take full responsibility, yet building in shame resilience.
- To admit my lies with little ego or excuses.
- To look at my possible negative addictions.
- To be willing to do the mental work moment-by-moment and meditate regularly.
- To free any pent up fear energy with safe ways of expressing anger or old anger, resentment.
- To read and listen regularly to positive audio information.
- Cry laugh and open my heart to attracting the right people to assist me on a tough inner and outer journey.
- Write and look at where in my past life the emotional patterns and beliefs emerged, so I can change and grow positively.

So here goes...

My old story

As I grew through the years, I became depressed. I was so critical of myself and everyone, I saw life through the beliefs of a hurt child and an internalized "critical drama parent". People avoided me because my pain radiated everywhere. One of my spiritual teachers, early in my second marriage, said quite strongly: "When you leave the room, Roger, the light comes on!" I wanted to kick him. He didn't know how much I suffered. Now I realize he was doing his best to shake me out of being such a victim to my story or my conditioning. I had no real awareness or tools to make a paradigm shift in consciousness.

I judged others and myself with such mistrust—a "delightful" negative family pattern that has taken years to dissolve.

I lived with an internalized lie. I remember my father saying repeatedly from his own hurt childhood: "Never trust anyone, son! Hit first in a fight, never cry, and never show your vulnerability by crying! Big boys don't cry!" Well this big boy wants to be truthful and vulnerable and certainly cries inwardly, and at times, outwardly.

What starts an inner journey?

There are many situations that can trigger an inner journey. For some it may be as simple as taking yoga lessons, or as devastating as the deep shock of having a "dis-ease" like Cancer. It could be hearing a sentence like, "Change your thoughts change your life." Or having an abortion, or getting married and realizing after the honeymoon you don't know why you married. It could be attending a course on personal growth or going to a counselor to talk about a partner dying or leaving you. For many it could be flashbacks to what happened in childhood. It could even be a whole combination! The Universe is always your teacher. However, I often did not want to learn!

For me, the trigger was a book. When I read famous psychotherapist Carl Rogers' book *On Personal Power* I cried inside over his approach to listening to hurt, angry people and helping them heal. He touched my reality in a way that even I did not understand. I would have loved him as a father figure. (I think millions around the Earth did!) His influence was the beginning of my wanting to grow and find the "lost me!" I loved his book *Becoming Partners* (about marriage and its alternatives). In the chapter "Three Marriages—And One Growing Person" he asked one question to Irene (a person who had gone through three marriages) and then listened with no interruption. The wisdom and insights from Irene were amazing. What made me start to "break open" as a man and cry deep, heartfelt sobs released my inability to cry. What triggered the tears was a feeling of what I could have been and done if I had a very different understanding of self and life. Simply put, I felt no real love for others or myself.

Carl Rogers, and later metaphysical lecturer and teacher, Louise Hay, helped me look into the mirror of my life and see the "black ball" parts of me that I have despised; and love them!

I realize now, those parts of my past have been vital ingredients to my becoming whole, healed, and creative. This has happened through my learning to love and forgive, even when others may still judge me harshly. I now have learned to say and believe: "I cannot afford the false luxury of their negative thoughts!"

As I write, I realize the importance of "beckoning intent", a concept developed by Carlos Castaneda. I am reminded of Wayne Dyer's book, *The Power of Intention,* in which he quotes from Castaneda's book, *The Active Side of Infinity.* Wayne read this just before undergoing successful surgery on his artery:

> *Intent is a force that exists in the universe. When sorcerers (those who live in the Source) beckon intent, it comes to them and sets up the path for attainment, which means that sorcerers always accomplish what they set out to do.*

I want to invite and live in the Source in this time of personal pain, and I want to retain this integrity in the rest of my life so I can learn and teach. I experience the Source when I meditate. Where I learn to listen with an open heart!

When I am truly listened to by Source it's like a close friend. I feel my eyes water, and my inner power of wisdom rises up into awareness. Then what I face in life feels like lessons to be learned. I believe this: that to give a person the gift of being truly listened to, can enrich love and inspiration for living. I experience this *listening power* in self-help groups, where Source is working to help each other listen with such *warrior* love. I love such intimacy.

In the early days, as I started to grow, I was naive. I saw some counselors, and what unraveled was the revelation of my fear of life and that I had been living my life without any true understanding of love ... the love inside me. This man's—this hurt boy's—rage at his own upbringing came through with such venom! I grew up scared to feel how scared I was. Have you experienced fear dominating your life? Fear of self and of life, I believe, this anxiety kills us early and attracts a lot of destruction into our lives. I see this so often in men as they open their mouths to speak about how they live life. The beliefs and feelings of mistrust and rage surface so quickly. Even in men who appear so knowledgeable, cynicism breaks their hearts. So let's do our lives differently!

DIVE

2

‹⌒›

Dare to be me: *Warrior* Love

As I sit looking down the mountain and at the deep blue sky I ask myself:

Do I really want to change and grow, or am I too fearful of what I may find? The answer comes:

Dare to be you; not what you think others may want you to be!

This is where a retreat into your wisdom and love can begin. This book is from my heart—nonacademic and written in simple language. It is about what I have learned to love, especially the power within, which watches my negative self-destructive thoughts and behavior, and feeds my intuition positively. It invited me to "come out" to Crete (before I leave this training ground called Earth!) So here goes. Hold onto our magical carpet and fly with me!

Don't die wondering—life is a series of lessons

What if you and I left this life knowing who we are and that we are full of love, kindness, and creativity? What a wonderful thought! Imagine … no bitterness no regrets. No unnecessary disease. We learn to open our *inner power* to see life as constant learning and a loving place to be.

I know I am not perfect, and I have made mistakes. The mistakes attract tough experiences, yet I see everything as lessons that teach me about authentic compassion and self-compassion. This, in turn, carves out my unique path towards consciousness and transformation.

Now imagine being at our own funeral

I ask myself: "How will I be remembered and spoken about at my funeral?" I immediately think that joy and inner peace would radiate to all who spoke about me at my funeral. Yes, there may be some people who might say, "What a lovely rogue he was," yet it would be said with love for my imperfections. Because I allowed myself to love myself from a place of authenticity, I may have been hurt. I may have transferred my pain onto others, risking the path of loving and being loved! I may have hidden parts of my life from those close to me, and I might take this with me to my maker! Some people may stay silent for fear of offending my name and others may gossip their opinions. Yet no matter, I would have lived with love in my heart.

Well, I make a clear choice to share those hidden thoughts with you in this book. I ask you to go deep into resonating with your own life as I unravel mine. I sense, then, that the hidden forces, faculties and talents, become alive as I discover myself in being truthful, without fear of criticism, gossip, shame, or blame.

Risk loving you

Now, to risk loving means loving my more permanent self enough to be truly human and at times become excruciatingly vulnerable and intimate with the images that the mirror of life reflects back to me. Yet I do so with self-compassion. I know I risk everything I have ever helped to create back home by being truthful. I am not writing this book to hurt anyone. I am writing it to, just maybe, help you, the reader, be more open to change and go within to experience with me some realization of:

Who am I?
What do I need to learn?
What have I deep inside to give?
What is my real purpose in this life?

Often I hear from people what they *don't* want; yet not what they love with passion, the latter I believe, can expand our capacity for unconditional love. This is probably the only capacity we take to our next life in spirit. That may be a little advanced for you to comprehend at this stage; indeed, when I first heard this I said, "Get real. Life is tough. It's not about learning unconditional love!"

Yes, that was my first reaction to being asked to love *me*, a man! All I know is that, when someone suggested, "You can learn to love *you* just as you are." I scoffed so hard I choked. My resistance was so full of cynicism. I thought I was a hardened, "street-wise" man with life's knocks to prove it! I loathed being open, and I had no real emotional language or intelligence. I was a "man!" Ah! What a limiting belief! Ring any bells, men?

So now on day one of a thirty-day quest in Crete, I start this book sitting in an isolated villa, high above a town in the southern part of the island, with the morning sun warming my typing fingers. Outside, Konstantina, my landlady, is gardening with her beloved long-haired black Collie dog, ReBell! The villa took ten years to complete… that's Greek time… slowly, slowly! In Greek, *ciga ciga*!'

First Morning

At home in the UK, I begin the day by sending a text—a positive affirmation each day—to a hundred people or more. It's a lovely action that inspires me. Now being abroad, I give a positive affirmation to myself from Louise Hay's pack of *Wisdom Cards*. The card says, *"I can heal myself on all levels!"* And on the reverse side it says: *"Healing means to make whole and to accept all parts of myself, not just parts I like, but all of me."* How appropriate. And then I open her book, *You Can Heal Your Life* to a random page and read: *"My life doesn't work."* I am reminded how I used to wake up saying, "My body, finances, and relationships don't work!"

Now I have manifested a beautiful villa with a magnificent view of a winding snake-like road between sun-scorched mountains and the sea. I can hear goats—their bells are ringing. And I can hear dogs barking.

The most precious gift is time to think and write this book, away from all family and friends. It is my retreat to all my earthly senses and with the unseen inspiration calling me and guiding me. Let me dive in the deep end. As Dr. Deborah Anapol wrote, *"Love is its own law."*

I accept love is a mystery and most people want love.

Here is what I have learned over years as I have grown to like and gradually love *me* and life, that I call *warrior* love.

- I have confidence in my ability to communicate to a whole range of people. They often share their secrets and their willingness (and resistance) to love themselves.
- I am learning to be a giver as well as a receiver of love, with a high degree of compassion and self-compassion.
- I do my best not to judge or gossip. The effect of gossip is so destructive; when I see myself do it, I do my best to stop.
- I am a person learning to have pleasure, including sex, without shame.
- I am allowing others to love me in deep platonic friendships. This was one of the most difficult changes, because I never thought or felt loveable.
- I am learning to take back my power to earn good money doing work I love. I realize now how important this is toward building self-esteem, self-worth, and self-love.
- I am learning to say positive affirmations in the mirror about my mind and body and soul, including my sexuality. I love playing audio principles of success daily, especially when I find myself reverting to old negative habits.
- I am learning to follow my intuition by meditating.
- I am willing to learn from teachers who cross my path.
- I am learning to turn my negative beliefs into positive affirmations: Examples:
  "I am open and receptive to all good!"
  "I am safe."
  "I release the need to be right."
  "I am at peace. I love and approve of myself."

- I am learning, gradually, to let people know who is behind the masked, hurt adult and releasing the "genius" child. I believe this genius is in all of us—when we choose to love ourselves by developing a nurturing inner parent! A parent that loves us, even when we make mistakes—especially while we learn. This makes *warrior love* a reality.

- I am willing to let go with love, relationships that constantly criticize and try to control me through guilt. I ask myself: What in me attracted this experience? I take responsibility to do some work to change and heal *me*.

- I am learning gradually to tell the truth by courageously *owning* my story.

- I realize that, as I learn to love myself, I can forgive myself, especially when I take responsibility for my mistakes.

- When I look into a real mirror or a metaphorical mirror that reflects what I have attracted to me in experiences, I can now learn patience and believe myself when I say, "I love you, Roger, even when you make mistakes." I am learning to be patient—not an easy family pattern to change. So often I have wanted to jump a whole series of lessons, because my ego wanted everything *now* without doing the work.

- Most importantly, I ask people I have hurt to forgive me, and I ask this with authenticity.

- I am learning that, when I invite the source of love to help me, even the toughest experiences are transformed into healing.

- I am learning to handle anger, jealousy, guilt, shame, and grief, and see each of these emotional states as an opportunity to learn.

- I am learning the difference between man-made laws of love and natural laws of love.

- I see more clearly that to have a real relationship with another, I need a shared life purpose and similar spiritual values.

- I am learning what I need in a relationship. This is an emotional resonance of appreciation for self and each other based on being true to self and the other person. Then criticism is so rare, and each day can be full of love and happiness.

- If the relationship is built just on sexual attraction, and an unwillingness to truly love one's true self, then the relationship with self and anyone else is a co-creation of unhappiness.
- I am willing to live on my own and be happy rather than accommodate fear, guilt, shame, and resentment from another.

And now, I dive into that part of me that wants to stay secret!

How to let go without making *me* wrong or *me* right

Now my aim is to manage the change and transition with my primary partner with deep gratitude, love, and integrity. Some of those changes are personal to us. Simply, we have changed, and we need to go our different ways and do what our spiritual paths guide us to be. Like many partners, we gradually learned to take each other for granted. We did things often separately; we lost the zest for being together. Our hobbies were so different. What we agree on, however, is that we want the best for each other. If I am in a prison of self-righteousness and the other is wrong, then it's still a prison! I want to be human not right!

For years I have loved and sat listening to my partner, and she has done the same for me. We always gave the gift of deep listening to each other. We have talked at length in the later years about our relationship and whether to "open" our marriage to others, which I later suggest can be such a gift of love to similar-minded partners. The problem is, when we have been conditioned to monogamy, then being open can be so hard, because thoughts of guilt, fear, and criticism, can erase love of self and our own self-compassion. I loved faithfully as a monogamous man, until some years ago. And somewhere, I chose not to tell my primary partner that my capacity for love was expanding in a way that was new and not fully understood by me. As I write this book, I still love her deeply. Yet our energy vibrations are so different, and our way of understanding marriage has changed.

Constant self-criticism, I believe, kills love

I saw constant signs of my partner not loving and accepting how beautiful she is, and her self-criticism hurt me so much. No matter how much I appreciated and loved her, I came to feel that the blame she accepted of herself was my fault. What I experienced was growing anger inside her, especially when her mother died.

Insight: When you have experienced anger and criticism for, and from, a parent, that is unresolved, you may bring this emotional pattern into intimate relationships. I did blame my parents, and I take responsibility that this negative emotional pattern developed beliefs and emotions that I allowed to control me. I now choose to forgive my mother and father and not stay in blame. I cannot change anyone else, especially my partner. I need to change and be a person congruent to my beliefs. Hopefully, I am choosing to love, be loving and loveable. Constant criticism in any guise creates a vibration that brings ill health and constant resistance to loving self.

The mirrors

I consistently do a lot of mirror work, seeing what in me made my partner so critical of herself and, at times, of me. Now I accept that my love was not honest and good enough. I was not impeccable with my word. Sometimes I certainly took things personally, and I did not always do my best. And I made the assumption that I could go elsewhere to meet some of my needs.

So now I recognize that there is a beginning, middle, and an end in our intimate relationship. I recognize that people come into our lives for a time and then leave at the right time. It has taken us, as happens with so many couples, a personal crisis to separate. We agreed for most of our relationship to be monogamous. Then as both of our needs changed we grew apart and we met our needs in different ways. My partner clearly wants now to stay monogamous. I choose differently. I want to be open to whatever happens that is wholesome and does not make me wrong or my partner wrong. That would come from such unresolved pain and limiting beliefs. This is work in progress. I want to be gentle as I learn from our parting. I don't want to stay in the role of guilty person. Love for me cannot be turned on as a reward. It cannot be turned off as a punishment.

I would choose to live on my own and be happy rather than stay in a relationship where we both feel wrong

This is one great benefit of living by myself in a retreat and seeing the negative emotional patterns more clearly. It's painful to admit this, and yet so freeing. I just picked up *The Seven Natural Laws of Love* by Dr. Deborah Anapol and read: *"You are the source of love. You! Not your husband or your wife, not your lover, not your parents, nor your guru… love is within each of us and radiates outwards."* Over the years of struggling with where and what is love? I realize it's an *inside job!* that can be a truly worthwhile journey.

A lighter story! (But let me be clear—I am now not looking for the *perfect woman*).

A Sufi Story

> *Nasrudin met an old friend whom he had not seen for twenty years. They sat together in the cafe and talked over old times.*

"Did you ever get married, Nasrudin?" asked the friend.

"No, I'm afraid I didn't."

"Why not? I've been married many years, and I've never regretted it."

"Well," said Nasrudin, "I was always looking for the perfect woman. I wanted my wife to be beautiful, intelligent, and sensible."

"And you never found her?"

"I thought I had, when I was twenty. Her name was Ablah. She was beautiful, just the kind of woman I like, but I'm afraid she wasn't very intelligent, and her language was atrocious! I was embarrassed to be with her! She certainly wasn't the perfect woman."

"Was she your girlfriend?"

"No. When I was twenty-five I met a woman called Bahira. She was good looking and intelligent, but she wasn't very sensible. She spent all my money on frivolous things, and she couldn't even boil an egg! She wasn't the perfect woman either."

"Were there anymore?"

"Only one. At thirty I met Haddiyah, and she was truly a gift from God! She was the most beautiful woman I'd ever seen, and the most intelligent. What's more she was prudent and sensible, a good cook, and a brilliant conversationalist."

"She sounds like the perfect woman you were looking for!"

"She was the perfect woman I was looking for."

"Then why didn't you marry her?"

"Unfortunately, she was looking for the perfect man!"

Insight: I admit I was, in the past, looking for the perfect woman to marry and be monogamous for life; I thought the "perfect woman" would make up for my deficiencies and make me happy! I wanted to be the dominant male and have no competitors from other males. Oh what limiting beliefs! I needed to do a whole lot of work on my father-son emotional sexual patterns. I'll talk about this later.

New insights from the "emerging me"

I recognize how much I desire close psychological contact with others. I recognize how much I need to care deeply for another and to receive that kind of caring in return. I recognize, rather dimly, that my deep involvement in counseling was a cautious way of meeting this need for intimacy without risking too much of myself. Now I feel a whole new depth of *me* can be gained if I dare to risk giving more of myself. A capacity for intimacy has attracted hurt, yet an even greater share of joy, laughter, and love. I realize now that my hurt is a sign of being open and receptive to healing and learning. I may trigger someone else's hurt if I am intimate with that person. However, I am not always responsible for his or her painful feelings.

How has this affected my behavior? I have developed more intimate relationships with men. I can now share with men, and listen to men, on becoming more aware and conscious. I loved hearing from one man in a Heal Your Life group, when he said: "Roger, you are so much easier to be with when you give of yourself just as you are; I trust you and feel I can risk being just *me*!"

I feel this new emerging *me* is an adventure, and I can be in much more intimate communication with women with whom I have platonic, however, psychologically intimate relationships, and these have tremendous meaning and purpose for me. With these people I can share many aspects of myself—the painful, joyful, crazy, and egotistical parts of me.

Becoming a transparent congruent person

When I hide any deep personal change in me from others, whom I want to be intimate with, it opens a wound in my heart and also in the person's heart that I love. (Because I know intuitively when my partner makes love to another, I know somewhere in my soul this has happened.) So then my body tells me, *it's time to tell the truth*, but somehow I rationalize the falseness I feel, and tell myself it will go away. Then the dis-ease in my mind, body and soul can become worse and my body shouts to my mind, *tell the truth.* One of those truth's is me becoming a man who loves intimacy, that includes consensual sex with another (but I did not tell my primary partner). This secret has hurt my partner and I am truly sorry.

This action undoes trust in self and from those who love you. So now I face the truth and learn a much harder lesson. My wife is choosing to leave me. I have brought this upon myself and I take full responsibility for this. I want to learn warrior love that is honest right from the beginning and not hide that I am a natural polyamorous man.

Learning deeper lessons

This wrong action, I believe, is showing me many more lessons of how I need to become more honest about my ability to love more than one person. So the hard lesson of my betrayal is to lead to deeper awareness. Have you experienced this in your life - where what seems so wrong can turn into something that many humans could learn? Because we know we humans appear separate, yet we are all connected. How many of you could be honest and say or admit, *"I am able to love and be loved by more than one person, and that love could just be for sex, while in a primary relationship"*? I will return to this in Dive 3.

Now we are parting, and in some ways it feels a relief to be totally open to our individual truths and the different values and realities of how we experience life. I seek forgiveness; I want to forgive my partner *and* myself. Society may make me the guilty party. However, the truth is we may have hurt each other, but we have done a lot of work on ourselves not to prolong that hurt. We both want to part with love and not accuse each other, or make each other and ourselves wrong or "bad"! There may be some dark soul-searching nights for my partner and me. I know that anyone who wants to teach and be authentic goes through his or her own dark layers of secrets, fears, and guilt.

21

Facing my mistakes

Let me quote Wayne Dyer, in his role in the film *The Shift*:

I've found that every spiritual advance I've made was preceded by some sort of a fall—in fact, it's almost a universal law that a fall of some kind precedes a major shift.

And he adds so poignantly:

A fall can be an embarrassing event that reveals the exaggerated influence of ego has been allowed to play in one's life.

Awareness: Guilt can make me feel inferior. Many times people have tried to manipulate me by putting me in the position of being wrong. My parents, sisters, teachers, and ex partners did that. I admit I attracted those types of relationships. I now want to explain to my grown up children that *"my negative emotional patterns learnt in my childhood, have nothing to do with them and their inner worth."* It's important how they see themselves in a positive light.

I also realize I don't want to live under a "cloud" of guilt with my grown-up children or with my ex-partner. If I allow guilt to control my life, I deny myself love and stay stuck, so I admit my true mistakes and honestly say, "I'm sorry," from my heart. I now want to forgive myself and learn to be honest, open, and receptive to all love that life has to offer.

The true benefits of parting with love and forgiveness are that we will both take our capacity to love into the future, appreciating each other and ourselves from a place of expansion and unconditional love. We have so many possibilities with increased awareness and consciousness to attract what we truly want and need. We will also attract positive relationships that are honest and open. We are honoring our past love and taking good memories into the future, where we both have integrity. I want to stay friends with my ex-partner and will be there if she needs me. I see our parting as life giving us an opportunity to grow.

Choosing not to buy into fear!

Have you ever been at a place where you make out in your head that you're bad and your shame permeates everything you see and feel and you're losing every close relationship and everybody's respect? Well those are victim thoughts, and victims seek to be rescued, and then they seek to blame. This is such a waste of energy! I know I need to take full responsibility for my mistakes and the hurt those mistakes have caused. However, if I put myself on the cross (or let others do it), I will not learn to heal and be self-actualized with self-compassion. I also know this is time for deep learning. I learn to be assertive and not to be bullied by others or myself. (I suggest further reading: *Guiding Principles for Life Beyond Victim Consciousness* by Lynne Forrest with Eileen Meagher.)

Leaving a relationship after twenty-seven years causes hurt, pain, regret, and anger. Yet with continual willpower to forgive and let go with love, huge growth, I believe, can take place—even on the subtle cellular level. When I leave people, I often say, "Take good risks." So many of us say, "Take care." Well, I am doing my best to put those thoughts together. I need to "take good risks" in writing this book with deep discerning wisdom. I don't see that I am washing my "dirty laundry" in public. I see as I move forward with a positive intention that you and I can learn, and we can create a true healing on many levels. Initially, I did not welcome this inner journey. Now I welcome the inspiration of my inner calling that believes both of us, my partner and I, will grow in wisdom, trust and expand with creativity and kindness.

American spiritual teacher Vernon Howard wrote, *"Disillusionment with yourself must precede enlightenment."*

I do not want to excuse myself, yet I want to make sense to myself about how I have got myself into this situation. So many people learn to lie to themselves and their loved ones. Even people who appear to have the moral high ground do this. Is lying endemic to get on and have your needs met? *No!*

So many of us hold secrets in our family lives and our public lives that can literally kill us; it certainly kills love. Men in highly powerful positions in politics and business have learned to lie and cover up until money markets crash and scandals of fraud are exposed. I have just come from a chance meeting with a very voluble Englishman whom I met while I was relaxing in a coffee bar here in Crete. He realized I was English. (I was wearing a green hat!) After ten minutes of talking, this man looked frightened when I asked: "What was your work before retiring?" It was just an innocent question... a common way we men talk about work! His nervous answer came:

"I used to teach Swiss bankers English in Berne." he replied, looking over his shoulder as though really frightened. Then, in a soft tone he whispered, "I have never met such a bunch of morally corrupt people in all my life. I even got told off for introducing good ethics in my English class! All they are interested in is their rich cars and houses!" He left nervously, cycling fast down the high street, as though he was going to be assassinated!

Can we make a difference by being more open and truthful? Yes. If we are prepared to have courage, then we can inspire others to have courage to share their vulnerabilities. Which reminds me of the next story:

Starfish on the Beach

While walking along the beach one day, a young man noticed thousands of starfish had been washed up by the tide. The tide was going out, and the starfish were stranded. There was no way that they could get back to the water, and within an hour or so they would be dead.

In the distance, he noticed an elderly woman, who was picking up the starfish from the beach and throwing them back into the sea. He approached her and asked, "What are you doing?"

"I'm throwing these star fish back to the sea."

"But why are you bothering? There are thousands of them, and what you are doing won't make any difference," said the young man.

"It will make a difference to this one," said the lady as she hurled another starfish into the receding tide.

In my opinion, yes, we can learn to lie and die inside. Maybe there are millions of lies held on the beach of life, yet this lady's example is worth following. I want to own my unfolding truth and throw myself back into the sea of life and live and become open and receptive to a vast pipeline of new possibilities. I want to teach people—especially men who are willing—to love who they are and not control or be controlled by fear and all its accompanying emotional patterns.

Groomed fear from "threats"

One of the first things I remember my father repeatedly saying to me in our isolated country "madhouse" was one of the most undermining thoughts I have held in the heart of my life. I now know it came so much from his own abused childhood: "Roger, never let anyone know what you truly feel. You may never know when they will use it against you!"

I stop writing and go deep into the negative power of that one thought, which I repeated to myself as a child, as a teenager, and onward into adulthood as a daily subconscious mantra. That one thought creates such internal damage in mind, body, and soul! I immediately want to counteract it with a positive affirmation: "I trust all life. All life loves and supports me."

You see, I want to trust life and myself. I want to trust that, if I am increasingly honest in my feelings and about my story, life will heal me. I want to trust that there is truly a "divine mind"—a higher self—in all of us humans that respects truth when the power of intention is kindness, love, and truly sought forgiveness.

However, the original internalized thought from my father would say, "You're an idiot, Roger, for expecting people to forgive and love you for being truthful."

People might think, and possibly say to my face, that I am an idiot for being honest. Yet if fear meets fear what do you get? *More fear!* This is what appears to govern so much of our lives. I want this "journey to the power within" to replace fear with authentic love. When I love myself with fear, I think, *What are other people saying and thinking about me?* Then the *ego has a field day with me.* The ego wants to survive at the expense of truth and love. This creates loneliness and isolation. My wooden counseling hut (in my back garden) rings with the history of such yells of self-blame and blames of parents, partners, children, politicians, teachers... anyone! And this is what keeps the energy stuck in guilt, and guilt seeks punishment and punishment produces disease!

Insight: I believe boys who become men with the same type of negative affirmation that my father gave me, along with many more negative ideas planted firmly in their subconscious minds, can, on a large scale, create and attract wars, abuse, and slavery. On a smaller scale, they can attract all types of negative addictions. In addition, they are malleable in the hands of ideological fundamentalist religions and terrorist organizations that want to rule our world. Thought joins to thought. So, unless we change those destructive thoughts, our world will not be a safe place for us to love and be loveable. We men particularly need to change our conditioning. I believe we can take off our emotional and physical armor by being addicted to finding love inside ourselves, inside our hearts—mind, body and soul. I have often counseled men in particular who could have easily been fodder to violent angry organizations. Let me tell you a Hindu story:

Hiding the Secret

Many, many years ago, when the earth was young, the legends tell us that all human beings were like gods, but they became very haughty and proud, and so abused their god-like nature that Brahma, the chief god, decided to take it away from them and hide it where it could never be found. He called together a council of the lesser gods to ask their advice.

"I think we should hide it in some dark forest where human beings have never set foot," said one. "They will never find it there."

"Oh yes they will," replied Brahma. "One day, every mile of the earth will be colonized by human beings. They are sure to find it in a forest."

*"Then we must bury it deep in the earth," said another.
"They will never find it there."*

"Oh yes they will," said Brahma. "One day they will dig mines for gold and precious stones, and they will surely come across it in the earth."

"Then we must bury it in the ocean," advised a third. "The ocean is so vast that no human being will ever be able to explore its depths completely."

"Oh yes they will," said Brahma, becoming impatient with the poor advice. "One day they will build submarines and travel to the bottom of the deepest oceans. And before you suggest it, they'll find it on the highest mountain."

Suddenly, Brahma's face lit up. He had an idea. "I know what we'll do. I know where we can put it where it will never be found."

"Where's that?"

"Deep inside the human heart! Nobody will ever think of looking there!"

This story comes from Eric Butterworth's book, *Discover the Power Within You: A Guide to the Unexplored Depths Within.* For Butterworth and those who think like him—including Hindus, Sufis, Gnostics and Mystics—looking within to find God—or the Source—is the whole purpose of the spiritual life.

Awareness

You might choose to put this book down now and just meditate on what threats were given to you in life that made you so frightened of *you* and living your life with creative love. Also, reflect upon how those threatening thoughts have become deep beliefs that affected your life in relationships, parenting, work, money, sex, spirituality, health, and any area of your life.

Insight: So many of my clients have been groomed by threats that have disconnected them from the power within and have affected their ability to have self-worth, self-love, and self-esteem. I love the affirmation: "My thoughts are my best friends." Whenever I start on a real downer, I remember to say these powerful words. I imagine the crystals in my body, which is 70 percent water, becoming beautiful! Especially when I read Dr. Masaru Emoto: *The True Power of Water: Healing and Discovering.*

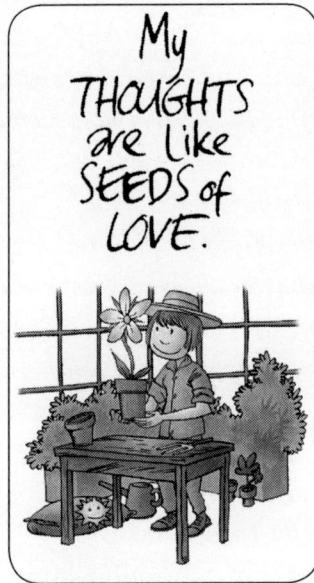

Early times

From a very young age, I knew only the fear of raised voices and the violence I heard in those screams. I was the youngest of three children. My mother wanted a boy after two girls. So at least I was wanted! (Unfortunately, many clients I have worked with felt they were rejected in the womb!)

When I see a photo of myself at nine months of age, on the lawn at home, I see looking back at me a very scared little boy who was going to do his best to survive. I chose a set of parents who were in a "war marriage." By this I mean that my father proposed to my mother when he was going off to war, which he never did. Instead, he went to Canada, where I think he met many women and realized his prowess as a sexual man; so he returned from the war, like so many men (and women) do, a very different man from the one who proposed to my mother. However, my mother was pregnant, and in those times the honorable thing had to be done.

Both parents had experienced a vast array of childhood abuse on both sides of their families, and this eventually played out in the way my sisters and I were parented It is interesting that I have spent forty-three years of my life listening to abused men and women. Is that why I chose my parents? And they chose me? I did find this difficult to accept—the fact that I actually chose my parents. (Many metaphysical teachers now believe that's how it happens). I do now see that my childhood experiences have assisted me in my work and hopefully helped me be non-judgmental and authentic to the hundreds of clients who chose me to unburden their stories and make sense of an old saying: "When you know the true history, everything makes sense!" It does not excuse wrong behavior of any kind, yet it can help us see the real person behind such poor actions. This reminds of the Buddhist story:

The Thief Who Became a Disciple

One evening, as Shichiri Kojun was saying his prayers, an intruder entered his house and, holding a big, sharp knife to the holy man's throat, demanded his money or his life. Shichiri, unruffled, said to the thief, "Don't disturb me. Can't you see I'm busy? There's some money in the draw over there. Take it!" Then Shichiri went on with his prayers. As the thief was stuffing the money in his pocket, Shichiri shouted. "Don't take it all. I've got some bills to pay tomorrow." The intruder, surprised at encountering such a strange response, left some money behind, and as he was leaving the house, Shichiri called after him, "Isn't it good manners to thank a person when he gives you something?"

"Thank you." said the thief, and off he went.

Some days later, the authorities caught the thief, and he confessed all his crimes, including his offence against Shichiri

> *Kojun. When Shichiri was called as a witness for the prosecution he said, "As far I'm concerned, this man is no thief. I gave him the money, and he thanked me for it." The man was jailed nevertheless, but on his release from prison he went to Shichiri and became his disciple."*

Insight: As I start to be impeccable with my word and watch what comes out of my mouth, I begin to know that I want to be a disciplined, truthful person, and I believe deep down most people want that for themselves. When we share our own vulnerabilities, a healing space is created where "unconscious behavior" becomes conscious. Then transformation can take place on physical, mental, emotional, and spiritual levels. I discover this "person-centered power within" repeatedly in self-help groups and counseling. Choice then becomes increasingly conscious.

Do it now! Let go! Dissolve the emotional charge with love and forgiveness! Be willing to practice and practice, telling the truth to yourself in the mirror then to the people who truly matter.

Our parents are always doing their best with the awareness they have. Returning to the story of my parents. In the 1950s and '60s, divorce was an expensive option for my father and mother. They had very little money, and both must have realized they were trapped and certainly had been duped into thinking that marriage was what they truly had wanted. My father moved us, when I was born, to an isolated, run-down country house with a low, beamed ceiling. There was nobody around to hear the screams. He said: "I love the countryside." Yet he really wanted a kind of freedom. He put us, "out of sight and out of mind!"

Consequently, my parents argued most often at night, and we could hear this rage through paper-thin walls. During the day, my father would be at work, or as my mother would say sarcastically, "off with his waitress." Oh, how I hated my mother and father being so sarcastic; their voices scorched my soul.

My father, a clever man, ran a café, a job that he felt was so much beneath his abilities; but he needed to pay the taxman from a war debt.

Insight: When a parent literally hates what he or she does for a living, that rage can so easily spill over into every area of life, especially loving relationships and parenting. Just hearing parents talk about work they bitterly resent, I believe, makes a child cringe with fear and physical ailments often follow… I do believe I always had hearing problems because I never wanted to hear what became a daily dose of negativity from parents and my sister's sarcastic arguments.

Suggestion: To help me write this now, I love saying or singing the affirmation below to great music and dancing with arms open. Then I put my own arms around *me*. It's like saying to the universe: "I am ready!" Here is the card from Louise Hay's *Wisdom Cards* that picked me: *"I am willing to change and grow. When I am ready to make positive changes in my life, I attract whatever I need to help me."*

The subconscious mind remembers everything—it cannot take a joke!

The trauma we three children were forced to listen to ended up having effects on all our future relationships, but most of all on how fear and anger dominated our emotions! My mother's emotional weapon was a face that could kill at fifty paces, linked with long silences as a weapon. She could punish us all by her sharp tongue that often screamed with the torture that flared inside her at the slightest provocation. This we suffered repeatedly day after day and year after year. No wonder we were all so angry; that was our experience.

As I write this I say, "I am safe!" It helps me know I am protected as I write what comes next.

Trauma attracts trauma

My mother had various emotional breakdowns. When I was seven years old, I found her overdosed. I felt powerless and wondered what I had done wrong! She was sent into the local "psychiatric bin," was given electroconvulsive therapy (ECT), and came out not knowing my name.

I was horrified. And what made it worse was that my mother knew my father was off with one of his women. She could not take the pain of her jealousy. I remember my father covering up my mother's cry for help to the local doctor, who certified my mother insane without even talking to her. I was in my bedroom, and heard my father say, "I have no idea why Tiny [her nickname] took an overdose; she has so much to be happy about!" I wanted to kill him! Not an easy feeling to carry as a child.

Yet we three children knew. No truth, just a cover up. How often do we all do this in dysfunctional families? I have heard this situation so often from clients. During my years as a social worker, I met many, many parents who could be so brutal to each other and their children. Luckily, nobody on my watch died!

I once said to the ex-minster of heath, David Ennals, whom I was lucky to work with, "So often the wrong people are in mental institutions." He was confused until I asked him to read the book: *Sanity, Madness and the Family: Families of Schizophrenics* by R. D. Laing.

Do read this book. It's a classic that shows that the most sensitive persons in a family are persecuted and become the "scapegoats" for the "sins" or "craziness" of the family. Often people were put in mental institutions, which I visited as a field officer of MIND (a mental health charity in the UK). I saw at firsthand what hellish environments were given to patients, as so-called caring treatment for such souls. People often stayed for years in these hellholes that should never have been there. (I don't like the word *should*, yet I feel it's appropriate in this context.)

David Ennals and I worked together as part of a team to start the MIND campaign that is still going today. The simple aim was to assist people who return to the community after what I call "a break open to their truth"—otherwise known as a "breakdown"!

The danger of unintentional yet harmful childhood internalized labels

My mother labeled my father a "womanizer," and whenever she told me off, she added: "You're just like your father!" I don't think she was even aware of what she was saying. This crucified me inside and still sends reverberations throughout my body. Her anger at my father skewed my thoughts and convinced me that I would grow up like my father. At first I did not compute what a "womanizer" was. All I knew was that it made my mother unhappy. I learned to take in negative thoughts so early into my mind and body that I shut off from anyone who came close.

Insight: When anger is your daily dose, you rationalize the world as an angry place. The lens of your mind, body, and soul becomes contaminated. And so you recreate that negativity in thought, word, or deed!

I love the affirmation: "I clean the windows of my mind, body, and soul with gentle love and forgiveness." You may think I am crazy, but I am singing this right now to the mountains and the goats outside my door.

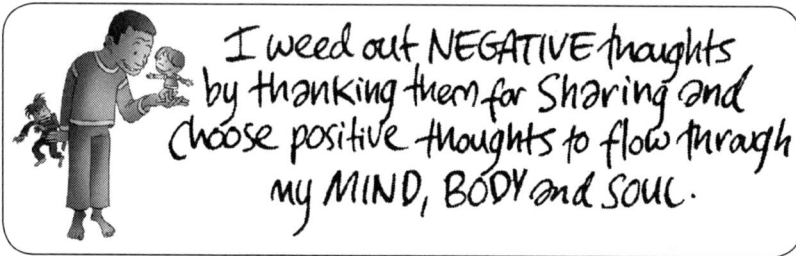

I weed out NEGATIVE thoughts by thanking them for sharing and choose positive thoughts to flow through my MIND, BODY and SOUL.

Trauma attracted trauma at school

At school I was caned a lot. I thought I was a dunce. On my first day at school, I cried when I left my mother at the school gate. For that, I was put in the corner with a dunce hat on. Wow! What a caring, loving start that was!

Please hear this: I do not want you to feel sorry for me. I am just saying how it was. At school I learned not how to learn, but how to survive!

Insight: So many children's genius is being lost today. They are being forced to learn with such conservative and competitive methods. Teachers, who are often my clients, come to counseling exhausted and often disillusioned from fear of being checked up on, by Ofsted (the official body for inspecting schools in the UK). This lack of trust together with a lack of person-centered, humane learning, is leading to fear. Paperwork is becoming more important than people, and more important than young people's true capacity for loving to learn. Although I do recognize we need some accountability in our school and college environments, this present method (in my opinion) doesn't seem to be working. The parasite of domestication is strong in our rigid school system. Because of this, alternatives have been born, like the [Rudolf Steiner] Waldorf humanistic approach and various home school models.

A lovely book that is timeless in wisdom, is Carl Rogers' *Freedom To Learn*. Another is John Holt's *How Children Fail*. I would like to see a book: *How Children Succeed with Love*!

Surviving school

I may have looked as though I was listening; yet I was dreaming: *There must be a better life than this!* I had no understanding of anything except how to survive school and my family. So often I was brought up in front of school as a boy who could not remember his poetry lines. I was like the boy Dibs who just got everyone's disapproval for poor behavior. Do read *Dibs in Search of Self* by Virginia Axline. She is a brilliant play therapist who brought a disturbed boy into his true genius.

I had no understanding of English grammar and would be caned for ranking bottom of my class in Latin. All I wanted to do was run … just run from school… and then run from *me* inside. I learned to bury feelings. I would not listen to them, and I would not show my vulnerable emotions. Yet the consequence was that I lied to everyone, including myself. I became an actor. My father's threat was coming true. I went to school with Chris Tarrant. He was head boy, and now is a TV millionaire. Chris often sent me for the cane to Major Wormal Headmaster, as I was always a rebel.

Nobody taught me ideas like this quote from Louise Hay: *"Life is really very simple. What we give out, we get back."*

Life got worse. I was bullied at my secondary school. After three years of humiliation, it got so bad that I turned on my bully and nearly strangled him. My father thought this was a good reaction. I became so scared of my anger. I believed I could kill if the right triggers were pulled! Well, readers, have you got any anger issues?

My anger sparked my imagination often during the night when I could hear my mother trying to resist my father, who felt he needed sex. As I said earlier, I used to imagine killing my father—not a very healthy emotional pattern. The nightly trauma certainly gave me a very warped idea of relationships between men and women. What was really crazy was my mother making me listen to her childhood stories of abuse while I was so young. This repeated trauma and emotional pattern of physical abuse has played out continually in my life.

Insight: I have listened with empathy to clients telling me what they think normal intimate sex should be like, and I have realized how abnormal these ideas really are. One ultra-religious, middle-aged woman who was very intelligent had rationalized being beaten before and after sex by her husband. She cried through tears asking me, "Isn't it normal? I have gone through this experience for years!" Oh, what we do to rationalize the irrational barbarity of what people allow to be done to their minds, bodies and souls. This is where fundamental religiosity can make an abused person feel so wrong for admitting they are being abused. I call this spiritual abuse of the worst kind.

Suggestion: Ask the person you love—a partner or a parent—what secrets have you had to hold from you or the world? Would it help to talk about them?

Abuse within the family

My mother's father, from a very young age, sexually abused my mother. These experiences made her hate sex and certainly distrust men. As I alluded to before, there was little experienced counseling in the 1950s, especially for the sexually abused. And the very idea of visiting a stranger to talk about private feelings made one appear to be a very "weak" person. Therapy or counseling was a luxury only the upper classes could afford. The financial barrier to poorer people is, I believe, still there.

Insight: When threats are used by an adult who is a parent or an authority over a child, and who is also that child's abuser, a great deal of internalized fear is brought about in that child, even as he or she grows into adulthood. So if I, another adult, suggest to that person to go within and love himself or herself, that inward journey can be full of initial terror! What horrors of memories may be encountered? To a person with that sort of abusive background, loving himself or herself can be like torture at first. I certainly think it was for me. I first needed to feel safe, then I had to trust I was strong enough to keep going. Now as I go within and find love, forgiveness, and freedom it's a whole different trip! I can now look into a mirror and be real when I say, "I love you, Roger." Even with all the mistakes I have made, I am free!

I have always yearned for freedom and at times that has been at a high personal price!

Learning to give and receive from the heart

I have often given away my services cheaply. I have asked people to pay me when they have made leaps in self-esteem or, with their new consciousness, so in turn help someone else who might need their assistance. Often I received financial help, and I had no way of paying back the money. I hope I have passed on this kindness later. This, I believe, is how life works in a more truly caring culture. Yet, as I said earlier, all of this undermined my own self-worth and my partner's opinion of me.

I have received such abundant finances through my father-in-law, and from my father and one sister, which I am so grateful for. Their help has allowed me to give my time and energy and skill to so many people. I was always grateful to my mother-in-law for suggesting, "Roger, you could build a special garden hut and use it as a place to meet your clients." Thank you ... may your spirit be free and happy.

That hut has attracted and heard such long stories from deeply frightened personalities, and I have been privileged to guide and witness deep and authentic positive healing.

Insight: Abuse in one generation does not have to pass onto the next generation and down the family tree. It can stop when people learn they are full of love, and not hate. However, this is a challenge we face today, right *now*. This little book is part of that offering. Imagine if all dictators had been loved and had been able to trust in their formative years. I don't believe they would come out from childhood projecting all their rage onto ethnic minorities or any group. I ask you, what would happen if all potential dictators and despotic leaders of gangs and tribes had learned to love themselves and had been taught love rather than hate and fear? What would our world be like? You might think that is so simplistic. Well, I have seen such positive changes in men who could be, and indeed were, so cruel to life.

Imagine in schools that we were taught *why and how to love ourselves.* What would our world be like?

Emotional patterns

As a child I listened to my mother rant and rave, but not to the wall, as the character in the film *Shirley Valentine* did. My mother's continual rants were at us children about what a bad man our father was and how trapped she felt looking after us in an isolated house. At times I remember how her crazy mood swings would even make our two large (often fighting) Alsatian dogs go under the table. When the debt collectors called on my parents, we all had to hide and allow the dogs to bark so our electricity was not cut off. How crazy we were. (This is a scene I am sure copied on many poor housing estates.) When people are poor in consciousness and money, they do the most desperate things.

How I attracted what I felt I deserved—and my way to defend myself was run or lie

I learned very young to survive three very angry women—my mother and my arguing sisters—by trying to appease them in a myriad of ways, which I still see surfacing in my emotional relationships with women. If I feel criticized by a woman with whom I am intimate, I want to run and hide. If I see a woman cry a lot, I feel myself shut off inside from my true feelings; I feel inadequate. I take full responsibility for attracting intimate relationships that are so often critical and full of anger. Now I am willing to dissolve that emotional vibration in me that I so traumatically learned from my mother's tears or rage. I am still working on this! Of course, in the past I have attracted relationships that were built upon similar emotional patterns. Now I have attracted a relationship that loves to give peace and genuine support and love. It is easy then for me to love from a place of freedom inside and out. It is so much easier not to hide behind lies for fear of risking anger and feeling so wrong. It is so refreshing to deserve positive and authentic love. I remember joking at my own expense to get attention from my family: "Nobody loves me!" What a crazy, damaging thought. I do regret this. I take *full responsibility* for this behavior. And I say a genuine, "I'm sorry," to my parting wife and children.

My father

My father became a man I could not truly love; he frightened me in so many ways, and I never trusted him. He always lied to everyone, including himself—and the taxman! Yet he was so creative. He was a genius when it came to building. He was just a very frustrated man— big physically—who learned to hit before he thought! He once admitted to me, "I can never change, Roger. I am my own worst enemy." What an affirmation! Somewhere, I think he knew how frightened I was of him, and that our relationship was based on fear and anger, even resentment. On birthdays he would sign the card: "As always, Dad." It used to make me wince inside. However, to be truthful he did once say, "My love, Father!" I remember that was a miracle.

On one of my visits home after listening to *The Power Is Within You* by Louise Hay, I remember asking my father, "How were you brought up, Dad?"

I listened and heard my father reel off a whole litany of harsh reality that he had gone through. He relayed it with no emotion; he just drank his brandy and sucked on his cigar a little harder. At the end, when he got near feelings and emotions, he said, "Oh, we must not dwell on the past; we have had a great life, haven't we, son?" I nearly cried in front of him.

Insight: When a son or daughter cannot trust a parent or both parents, it can be so hard later in life to feel true feelings and emotions. It's hard to identify real feelings, because it feels as if there are so many personalities floating through the conversations of your mind. I found it so hard to say, "I love you," to anyone—and certainly not to myself in the mirror. This is when my truth would become distorted and I learned to lie without ever feeling what love or truth is! My reality became so confused.

If you can, ask your parents: "What was your life like when you were growing up? How were you loved? How did your parents express love to you?"

These questions started the process through which I learned some of my father's background. I have now a much deeper compassion and forgiveness for his reactions to life. My own father's hatred of his masculine, alcoholic mother made him, I believe, desire intimacy with women. However, the intimacy became just for sex. Somehow he despised the women because deep down he wanted love. The one woman he did love, I believe, died of a heart attack. My father brought himself up, literally cooking his own meals and mending his own clothes. His inner distrust of his adult mother was covered in layers of anger. This was never resolved; he resented having to look after his mother as she grew old. His face would distort as he spoke to her with such resentment. The worst part was that she was deaf, and we all joked at her expense. I regret this. I often see this emotional pattern being repeated in grown-up "unloved children" who have lost respect for parents and who dread having to look after their elderly parents in their declining years. It is such a common emotional pattern in many western societies.

I know my father respected his own father, who spent most of his time trying to earn money to give my father and his older brother a better education. He did really have a true affection for his dad when he died. I remember him being soft and upset on the phone when he told me, "My dad has died!" I was on my honeymoon in Spain, and for once I wanted to hug him, but the distance prevented that from happening.

So I chose two parents who really were doing their best, with what they knew. However, life grew increasingly violent.

Violence

My reality was very precarious when I was a child. I would become hyper vigilant (like so many of my abused clients) to whatever was going on in the house. One minute all would be quiet, and then all hell would break loose, especially when my mother asked my father for money for school clothes. I can remember my feet hurting in shoes that were too small. My father owed many thousands of pounds in taxes to the Inland Revenue after he ran a gun factory during part of the war. His Jewish partner had taken the money and run. So Jewish people were no good according to my father! Oh, how unhealed hurt from unconscious parents can be passed down as prejudice to innocent children, often at mealtime. So many negative emotions and feelings are expressed during mealtime; no wonder poor food is often over eaten! Mealtimes are so full of undigested trauma in so many people who become obese or obsessively overweight later in life. Or the opposite: don't eat till you die—Anorexia. To lighten the mood, here's a humorous Jewish tale:

Stones or Bread?

A rich man went to see a holy rabbi one day and asked his advice on how he should live his life.

The rabbi questioned him about his lifestyle, before asking, "What's your diet like?"

"Very simple. I eat bread and drink water, and sometimes I take a little cheese, but I don't drink alcohol, and I don't eat meat," replied the man, a little pleased with his virtue.

"The first thing you must do is change your diet. You should eat some meat and drink the occasional glass of wine," advised the rabbi.

The rich man was shocked. He was very proud of his frugal diet and he protested, "Surely it is better not to live ostentatiously, and not to take more than my fair share of the earth's resources?"

But the rabbi was adamant, and he continued to tell the man that he had to eat more expensive food. When the man had gone, having reluctantly agreed to do what the rabbi had advised, the holy man's disciples asked their master, "What difference does it make whether he eats expensive food or simple food? Isn't it the man's own choice?"

"It makes a big difference," replied the rabbi. "If he is used to eating expensive food then he will understand that the poor people must have bread and cheese in order to live. But if he eats only bread and cheese, he will assume that the poor can survive on stones."

The emotional negative patterns between money and love

Sessions I have facilitated on the subject of money and prosperity reveal such emotive issues for people. They like and want money, and yet they hate it at the same time. Emotions related to abundance get so confused when they're mixed in with love and the lack of deserving. What were the rules of deserving around money and love in your household? For me there was never enough of either money or love. So, I grew up with the fear of never having enough of either, and this somewhere affected a lot of my choices in life. I never really believed that my love or my skills were worth much. How about you? I so often don't charge what my skills are worth. Well that is changing! It's so linked to low self-esteem.

How we make it up—how lies become our reality

When we are so unaware of how to heal our wounds of the past, we exaggerate the truth that comforts our traumas deep inside. As an example, my father would boast about how he never saw action in World War Two. I think his best time was being in the Royal Air Force. He constantly conjured up "absent without leave" stories at the dinner table. Then he would create a figment of illusion. I later heard, before he became ill, that he told his grandchildren that he was a war hero. But he used to boast to me that he never saw action.

Insight: When we lie to ourselves, we are always on alert and put our lives into compartments—hoping one area of life doesn't collide into another. This dilutes the good energy of love and inner peace and happiness. I know I can be in natural beauty, yet if I am lying to myself, I have an inner and outer face that reveals such fear of the truth coming out.

It takes a lot of energy to keep lies inside your heart— lies and regrets in our hearts contribute to aging

If, during our lives, we are unwilling to learn to find our love and lovability, when we get old we can become what I saw so often in homes for the elderly. Souls who have never really been truthful and have not learned to forgive their parents, and who have been bitter most of their lives, they lose dignity and are just drugged up to keep them alive in their pain. I remember one beautiful woman in a home I visited. She had such a strong sense of love and compassion. She visited fellow patients in their rooms and would listen to their moans and just smile and say very little. The lady just brought peace to everyone she sat with and in her time died a very peaceful death.

How do you want to die? And how do you want to live till then? These are important questions.

My father died at ninety, a very broken man with bowel Cancer. His ability to keep secrets in his life made him a very difficult man to get close to. One thing I am learning is that we cannot force change, and we cannot change anyone else. Change must come from the heart of each individual. I want to encourage you to trust yourself and the divine in you. It is a gift to let go of negative secrets and beliefs and learn to love *you*! Honesty and truth set you free to make authentic and happy connections with yourself and the world.

Heal your secrets now!

I see that when we hold secrets this creates an energy that never finds peace. Over time, secret lives become lies and eat away at us inside, through fear, guilt, shame, and resentment. Consequently, we can invite painful exits from this life. So I suggest to you, do the work now! Learn to love the parasite of fear right "out" of you. Don't leave it to your deathbed! Find love inside, and become ever so loveable! I promise it creates miracles of self-acceptance with deep appreciation. Do read the wonderful book, *The Voice of Knowledge* by Don Miquel Ruiz.

Both my parents were highly intelligent, yet had no inner awareness or wisdom of why and how they could change their lives for the better.

Suggestion: Read self-help books, go to groups, write and speak affirmations, meditate, learn new talents like dancing, let go of negative relationships in leisure time and at work. Attract new relationships! Learn about how to dissolve guilt and stop being a victim in every area of life. I feel this is worth repeating. Do read *Guiding Principles for Life Beyond Victim Consciousness* by Lynne Forrest. She clearly describes ways to come out of the *victim, rescuer, and persecutor triangle.*

Guilt: separation insurance

Sondra Ray puts it so succinctly in her book, *Loving Relationships*:

> *Guilt is the mafia of the mind. It is a protection plan you sell yourself to avoid anticipated punishment… (This is why guilt is always accompanied by resentment.) Guilt is the major obstacle to success in relationships. How can you let yourself receive unconditional love when you fear the consequences? How can you surrender to love when you fear loss? How can you give yourself what you most desire when deep down you feel unworthy?*

Later, she adds:

> *Imagine the consequences of believing that you being alive hurts your lovers! This one thought can cause you to suppress your feelings, withhold your joy, and deny your divinity for the sake of others. And if you are in love with someone special, you might even be willing to hurt yourself physically (and die) to protect your partner from aliveness.*

Don't concentrate only on how awful life is or was. I know you could say my story is doing that, but getting it out and owning it is part of the healing process. Write and own your story. This can help you let go of the person you think you're supposed to be and fully embrace who you truly are!

Insight: When I don't love myself, I put people I love in a "double bind." I always feel and talk in my head that I am not good enough for them, so whatever they say or do will never be right. In the end, either they leave, or I leave before they have a chance to.

Tip: Do regular affirmations, such as:

• I forgive myself for hurting others

- I forgive myself for letting others hurt me

Learn to meditate so the Divine can talk to you. Affirmations are you talking to the Divine! Play beautiful music. I am writing this to the heart-filled voices of "The Flower Duet" from the opera *Lakmé*. So entrancing!

Suggestion: After writing your story of gloom or doom, write a second story, but in this one, extract joy, no matter how small. You can *imagine* parents who loved and wanted you! Doing this changes your history. Memories are not *you* now.

Guilt is one of the biggest *bummers* that our mind can sell us. It serves no positive purpose! That will get your chatterbox going!

Imagine that your thoughts in this new story attract a new future and you live in the *now*!

Regret balanced by a gift from a dream

I admit I could not go to see my father before he died. Looking back, I realize I allowed my own fear to stop me. I regret this, but I am not going to beat myself up! Guilt never accomplishes real healing love. What did happen was that the Divine gave me a lovely gift. It was a dream that mother and father were both sitting on a rocking lounger, enjoying each other's company, with beautiful classical music playing, including opera, which they both loved here on Earth. And in the beautiful dream, a voice assured me: "They are fine; do not worry!" I woke up crying with joy and deep gratitude. Now, you may say that's merely an appeasement of my guilt. I say, "No!" Guilt creates fear. I let go of my fear and guilt with love and forgiveness!

Let's lighten up with an absurd funny story!

The Doctor's Diagnosis—A Sufi Tale

A man was in bed, very sick. He had not eaten or spoken for two days, and his wife thought the end was near, so she called the doctor.

The doctor gave the old man a very thorough physical examination. He looked at his tongue, lifted his eyelids to examine his eyes, listened to his chest through his stethoscope, tested his reflexes by hitting his knee with a little hammer, felt his pulse, looked in his ears, and took his temperature. Finally, he pulled the bed sheet over the man's head, pronounced, in somber tones, "I'm afraid your husband has been dead for two days."

At that moment, the old man pulled back the sheet, lifted his head slightly, and whispered anxiously: "No, dear, I'm still alive!"

The man's wife pushed his head back down again, covered him once more with the bed sheet, and snapped, "Be quiet! Who asked you? The doctor is an expert; he ought to know!"

Insight: We must never give our power away to those whom we think know more than we do. I had a leg injury from running, and I went to a doctor who said I required an operation. In his opinion, he doubted I would ever run or dance again. I said, "You are not going to touch my body. I will find someone who can help my healing without surgery." I did—a chiropractor. And in six weeks I was running. Now at sixty-five years of age, I dance each and every week.

DIVE

3

Healing all of me—the parts I have denied

I say out loud: *I am continuously in the process of change and unfolding my awareness, consciousness, and transformation. And so it is.* And my affirmation for today *Coming out:!*

I am possibly a hidden, yet natural, polyamorist—one who maintains more than one romantic relationship at a time. This is not a label I use easily to excuse hurting people I love. I want to understand the following questions: In my heart of hearts I do love my partner, yet why do I feel I want and need love from other women too, who love me just as I am? I have not groomed these relationships, and hopefully have not abused them. I ask sincerely, is it my hurt childhood emotional patterns that cause these needs? Is it a false need—some would say "warped" need—to fulfill love I never had? Is it that I love sex? Is it just the thrill of my ego loving attention? Is it an aging man just wanting attention? I truly want to understand how I can have so much love in me for women who show me love. As I write this I don't want to be seen as a tribal outcast. I am doing my best to be more aware; I am not just trying to excuse my actions. I do have feelings of love for all the women I have ever been with, and not just sexual feelings. I know I still love my primary partner, and we have had wonderful, passionate sex throughout our twenty-seven years.

I realize I have not faced these questions, and I am sure you may have ambivalent ideas about me. I want you to hear my heart; I am not trying to justify. I want to be open to a real understanding.

What is polyamory? I quote from Peter Bensons' book, *The Polyamory Handbook: A User's Guide:*

> *Polyamory is not a "license for affairs." The term "polyamory" from the Latin and Greek roots meaning "many loves." Means the practice or theory of having emotionally intimate relationships with more than one person simultaneously, with sex as a permissible expression of caring feelings, openly and honestly keeping one's primary (or dating partners) informed of other intimate involvements.*

He also says, *"Polyamorous relationships may be emotional without sex..."*

Polyamory is egalitarian between the genders (not sexist). It is so important for me to add what Peter says here: *"So polyamory is not about indiscriminate sex with many partners and it is not about secret affairs."*

This is what I flouted at the expense of my primary partner. And I am truly sorry. This is not an excuse. I do believe we are so conditioned to do this—both men and women: to lie about sharing love with other partners. If I could turn the clock back, I would tell my partner. This has shattered trust.

Now you know. Please suspend judgments. I touch the Earth with heartfelt regret!

I guess I can empathize with what it was like for people of many generations to be gay. I am possibly a polyamorist. There is no dictionary definition yet. I love to love different women, not necessarily sexually, who love me. I have covered up this need in me for years. I know therapists could say: "This is an addiction and needs treatment." and a possible reason could come from trying to cheer up mother and sisters! Maybe so. I choose not to beat myself up for this. I have learned that making myself wrong does not bring healing; it blocks my energy and wisdom. It's work in progress, and writing this book is helping. I hope you can find insights that assist you in healing and loving yourself and, most importantly, being more authentically you. I suspect the fundamentalist religious person reading this could have a "field day" of accusations. I ask you to let God judge me. Thank you.

Awareness leads to consciousness

Let me quote Deborah Anapol from her book, *The Seven Natural Laws of Love.* This is from the chapter on "Law of Truth":

> *The conditioning which most of us have gotten is the exact opposite of the law of truth. The man-made version could be stated like this: If you want to be loved you must project an image of perfection and never say anything, which might hurt someone's feelings. Never show weakness and never be impolite. Never reveal family secrets. Lie if you need to in order to make a good impression, and keep quiet about anything controversial. If you have been trained to lie about your real feelings and needs from an early age, being truly intimate maybe a challenge for you.*
>
> *The aversion to truth-telling is partly habit, but it persists for two reasons: First, in order to speak the truth, you have to know the truth. Second, you have to give up trying to control the outcome of speaking the truth.*

And Anapol adds so poignantly:

> *The best way to lie to others is to lie to oneself. After many years of lying to yourself, you may no longer know your true feelings and thoughts…You want to be authentic but you've forgotten how.*

This really makes so much sense in my own experience and in the experiences of so many of my abused clients.

I have been accused of talking too much about sex and of being addicted to sex. What I do want is for readers to learn that there are other ways of having relationships that our Western culture keeps a lid on. In my opinion, much of our Western consciousness through years of religious indoctrination and "Victorian morality" has forced us to keep secrets and not be truthful.

How does our culture see polyamory?

Counselors and therapists often know very little about polyamory (I certainly did not until I started to read books like Dr. Anapols's book *Polyamory in the 21st Century: Love and Intimacy with Multiple Partners.* I also attended a polyamory workshop in Greece.)

Many people may fall back on considering polyamory to be an aberration, a pathology to be avoided or "cured" (as people used to consider homosexuality). I quote from *The Polyamory Handbook* by Peter Benson:

> *A common myth in our predominantly Judeo-Christian culture in the Western hemisphere ... has been there is only one traditional or "standard" way, one valid and healthy and right way, for people to conduct their loving relationships and that is a pairing of one man and one woman.*

Questions I ask you and myself

I ask myself: Could I be covering up my pain by labeling myself a polyamorist? What payoff do I get from keeping secret this need that masks old wounds of loneliness, isolation, and deep rejection in childhood?"

Diving deeper: Am I rationalizing my irrational hurtful behavior?

Am I being so subtle that the ego (the parasite) of feeling unlovable, and it's a "dog eat dog world" where everyone is out to get me, means I must hide behind a label? Am I just seeking approval? Do I feel empty inside so I need others' approval?

I ask: Why are there so many painful, jealous divorces in our Western culture? Does this hide people's need for a new way to understand marriage, one of which could be polyamory? Could we change and share new relationships without divorces? Could we learn through loving ourselves to have more "open relationships" and still love our primary partners? Could an honest open relationship actually enhance the primary relationship? Please hear me; I am not saying all people need to be polyamorous, yet we need to advance our consciousness on this subject, or more and more people will hide and lie in unfulfilling marriages. So often people tell me they have had "affairs" and not told their partners. It's a scientific fact that we are, on average, living longer and we change in so many ways. These changes may include our sexual orientations and needs. What if our capacity to love ourselves makes us more attractive to others? I have no clear answers to any of these questions; my journey is work in progress. I have seen and experienced firsthand how hard life is for children who have divorced parents. I ask the question: Could humanity make a huge shift in consciousness and realize we are more naturally polyamorous than monogamous?

Imagine us being more honest and giving real respect to our main partner and our main partner to us, if we have emotional and possible sexual relationships, and all parties share together. I am not advocating sex with just anyone. I feel we would see less abuse, and we could actually create communities that are far more real and deeply therapeutic around emotions and sexuality. Children would have much more trust in parents that were listening and empathizing with all feelings. Children deserve to see and hear love rather than jealous fights and arguments between their parents. Imagine, instead of an increasing number of divorces, we could take responsibility for open relationships in which we have a primary partner, and our society and culture says "yes" to this type of behavior—if you communicate with deep integrity and you go at a rate that respects feelings and emotions of all involved! Being honest and truly caring when you have secondary relationships is being responsible.

I am asking this of us men especially: Can we learn to be open to being honest and truly caring if we feel genuine love for another women or man? Could *we* men allow that same freedom to our primary partner? I don't believe men come from Mars and women come from Venus. Can we learn a whole new way of being together that dissolves heart-wrenching jealousy and allows love and self-compassion to thrive?

Can we learn a new emotional language that really loves love? That is expansive rather than restrictive of our wholehearted way of being? I realize these are tough questions. I know we could make a safer world in which we could love ourselves and each other if we got the negative nonsense of our past conditioning out of the way. Could we learn how our *ego* so often defeats us in how expansive and deep love can be? Could we learn and truly experience Deborah Anapol's Seven Laws of Love? These are:

1. Love Is Its Own Law
2. The Law of Source
3. The Law of Attraction
4. The Law of Truth
5. The Law of Unity
6. The Law of Consciousness
7. The Law of Forgiveness

This book is so refreshing and could save so many loving relationships from ending poorly—or could we choose to keep love alive in all types of relationships.

Here is a quote from *The Prophet* by Kahil Gibran:

> *Speak to us of pleasure.*
> *Pleasure is a freedom-song.*
> *But it is not freedom.*
> *It is the blossoming of your desires …*
> *It is the caged taking wing … Ay in very truth, pleasure is a*
> *freedom song.*
> *… And some of your elders remember pleasures with regret like*
> *wrongs committed in drunkenness …*
> *They should remember their pleasures with gratitude, as they*
> *would the harvest of a summer.*

It finishes, *"People of Orphalese, be in your pleasure like the flowers and the bees."*

The music playing while I write this section is

"The Logical Song" by Supertramp and "When We Dance" by Sting.

I will later talk about open marriage. Well, reader, what I have said about myself may send your belief system going in all directions! I hope you can expand your heart and beliefs. I want to invite a much more open sharing between all people.

I want to honor feminine inspiration. David Deida puts it so well. I quote a small extract of the paradox I feel and experience from his book, *Finding God Through Sex: Awakening the One of Spirit Through the Two of Flesh*:

> *When I look at her, I am awed. Her beauty, her lusciousness, her smile, her eyes full of love, she makes my life worth living.*
>
> *When I look at her, I am repulsed. Her ugliness, her resistance, her anger. At times I want to be away from her, without her constant emotional twists and turns."*

Then later he states:

> *Altogether, nothing inspires me more than her. Her attractiveness pulls my heart, body, and mind toward her. I want to take her, make love with her, and enter her deeply, until we are both turned inside out in love.*

David goes on and ends:

> *The feminine form is incomparable beauty, to man and woman alike. All of nature is summarized in her body, her moods, her energy. We must honor the feminine in all her glory, dark and light, without getting lost in her...*

Insight: I feel so close to these twists and turns in my relationship to the beauty and the dark part of my own humanity. When I don't allow my soul to be fed by the love of meditating, using affirmations, and just having fun, I can concentrate on what is wrong. I love learning to love life, and learning to love *me*, because I begin to see beauty even when life is raw or tough. Today, right now, I want human contact even if it's not easy. To hear my partner's voice can fill me with wonder or foreboding. I know if I am tired I will not do my best to be there and truly understand or empathize. At other times I feel from my heart the "art of passionate relating." I know I can relate to a woman or man with authentic passion and truth from my heart.

Suggestion: Be brave and dive deep into the many levels of your vulnerable reality. Something that helps me is to list what I am feeling and believing. Then, with a little mirror, I can see my immediate resistance when I say: "I forgive you, Roger, for all that you have done that has hurt others." Then I experience anger, tears, and cries from my soul.

This is eventually so freeing, because I go back to the mirror and ask: "What do you need in order to love *you* right now?" I then get an honest answer. Maybe it's just a hug or a friendly voice down the telephone. Maybe it's a walk in beautiful countryside. Or time to sleep outside if it's warm, and nourish myself with good food. What I don't need is rescuing or listening to news or TV. So often I dance ... or masturbate and relieve the pressure and experience pleasure and self-love.

Diving deeper: love without the limits of our negative thinking.

I imagine, sometimes, how things would have been if my original family had been more enlightened. What if my father had been able to be honest and open about his childhood and realize his need for *constant* sex with women came from such hurts in his own childhood? What if my mother could have been helped to make real choices about her abusive background and heal her self-image and learn how to love herself? What if, instead of listening to their violent arguments, we children had experienced them cuddling and doing their best to heal their wounds, never running each other down in front of us? What if they listened to us three children appropriately with respectful sharing at meals? What if, when we cried, we were allowed to be real and not rejected? I remember that my son, Simon, felt so respected when my partner and I involved him in "time to think" sessions. He thought it was marvelous to be so open with his parents.

Imagine if at school we could share what our families are doing best to heal wounds around relationships and sex and any related emotional issues. This is so different from just teaching the mechanics of sex. That class time would be "honest time" for teachers to be facilitators of feelings. Teachers could be real humans to the children they teach. That "freedom to learn" is about questions: Who am I? What is love? It is an opportunity to learn the answer to the question: What inner language do we need to learn to develop love for others and ourselves? The books I have listed in the appendix could be on bookshelves in all places of learning. Imagine having teachers of metaphysics and other philosophies coming into schools and colleges, not just to teach, but listen to students. Imagine that yoga and much more holistic subjects were taught, especially courses in juicing and healthy organic cooking. Imagine that homework was to listen to a CD on loving relationships.

As I said earlier, some counselors who have a narrow view of relationships may consider that I have a "sexual addiction" that needs curing. And here is a list that I could involve in long-term therapy:

- I had little touch or love when growing up.
- Sex was all around me, yet often violent.
- Nobody talked honestly about what was going on in my family. Crazy hurt experiences were just felt and left unhealed, never to be talked about. (I am doing my best now to own my truth. I hope this can help you find your "wise courage.")
- A lecturer on a college trip abroad groomed me and raped me. From this one experience, my life imploded. What made it worse was that he and I never spoke about it, and this made me want to "prove" myself as a "man"! What a survival technique!

I have done a lot of healing in these areas, especially through some counseling and emotional freedom therapy (EFT). There is a film of me doing EFT on this rape experience on videotape in 2009 with Gwyneth Moss, an excellent emotional freedom therapist. (See appendix 11.)

I believe when we have a very hurt child inside, if we are threatened as an adult with love being withdrawn, very bizarre behavior can be triggered. When I was told, "Go elsewhere to meet your sexual needs." I became open to attracting another relationship to fulfill my needs.

Fear of saying "I love you."

I often ask clients at some point: "Were you ever told you were loved?" The hurt reply is immediately "no" or "you must be joking." Sometimes, even if words of love were said, they didn't believe them.

I remember sharing this once with one of my sisters, and she said, "I don't think we were ever told we were loved!"

The unresolved hurt comes when parents die

When our parents died within six weeks of each other, they had been parted for thirty years. So much hurt came to the surface for both of my sisters. They are both very clever, and each is successful in her particular way. I have made a choice not to be in contact, out of self-protection. I feel a miracle must happen before we die! So I affirm the miracle: "My sisters and I are divinely guided to become genuine friends, and we can authentically forgive each other for all hurt caused!"

Insight: Our legal system, sometimes, lives off people who don't know why or how to love their true selves. I believe if we loved ourselves from a place of truth and forgiveness, we would have courts of forgiveness and reconciliation.

A special meeting that changed my life

Meeting a woman called Jo Berry was such a heart-warming experience for me. I heard her speak with the ex-IRA bomber, Patrick McGee, who killed her father at the Brighton bombing. Both she and the ex-bomber were on stage, talking so honestly together, at a Leeds Peace forum. Reconciliation can happen with deep healing. Do watch the TED Talk on YouTube called: "Disarming with Empathy." It holds so much of what I believe in action about forgiveness!

When you understand someone else's story, you realize why and how people can commit dreadful acts of violence. When you transform your pain, you and I can choose to empathize with our adversaries. *When you know the true history everything makes sense.*

Jo Berry says on the website, *Building Bridges for Peace*: "I passionately believe that there is humanity in everyone, and every time we demonize the "other" we are delaying the onset of peace in this world."

DIVE

4

Completion connecting as equals: becoming friends with my mother

One brilliant healing for me was hearing my mother say to me, "Yes, darling, I can understand you can love more than one person!" I had asked her, "Do you think, Mum, that it's possible to love more than one person, with or without sex?" This insight came from a woman who used to be so jealous and full of hurt. Let me explain.

In the last three years of her life my mother and I talked weekly at Betty's, a lovely teashop in Harrogate, Yorkshire, where she was greeted so kindly. Although she was eventually confined to a wheelchair and a home for the elderly, her mind was sharp, and we shared with trust and a certain depth of honesty about our emotional family patterns. Often she asked me to forgive her for comparing me to my father. This was a vital healing moment for me, and I hope it was for her as well. It was healing just to hear her say, "Please forgive me, Roger!" Mother said it with such sincerity. And I replied, "I do, Mum!" People watching us in that rather posh tearoom as we shared our hearts so openly may have raised their eyebrows at the tears we shed over our chocolate éclairs!

I shared with my mother some of what I had learned from Louise Hay's books and from other mentors and teachers. My mum sat opened mouthed with tears in her eyes. "Oh, darling, I would love to have known what you know!" And she followed that comment with, "It was so frowned on in my day to love yourself and be strong and independent. I would have been a very different person. I would never have got married so young!" Mum did add, "There have been times since I left your father that I have been happy."

A special moment of a visiting angel

I remember asking my mother how she wanted to die. She looked across the table and past me and said in a completely peaceful trance, "Do you see the angel sitting there?" And it was like a presence sitting in a chair. In a real divine moment, she whispered: "I know I will be all right." We cried and held hands, then hugged like two equal spiritual souls. All fear and criticism was gone! I cry while I write this. I truly miss you, Mum. She died in March 2012.

These connections between two equal people were such a relief for me, and she admitted that she wished she had told my sisters and me that she had loved us. She blamed herself for the anger between her two daughters. Mother was so frightened of my sisters' anger and their anger at each other.

Insight: I often hear of the shock in grieving relatives of unresolved anger that has become resentment. This comes to the surface (so irrationally) when a mother or father is dying or has recently died. It's like all the unloved and unforgiving memories and feelings come to the surface.

Suggestion: Complete by deep sharing's, and by listening to each other without judgment, if you can before anyone dies. This gives the opportunity to resolve any issues with your family. I know I have some work to do.

Practice listening to parents

To have completed such a rich personal forgiveness with my mum over three years was such a healing for me. I love you, Mum!

Listening to my mother's story was so healing for many of the hurts that I carried. I cannot urge you enough to sit with at least one of your parents and ask what his or her life was like growing up. Just listen and appreciate him or her for being as honest as possible. So many of my clients have done this, and it truly has helped them. If the parents have died, I often suggest a "gestalt" chair technique to assist in putting together the pieces of a picture or puzzle of your life. The client first sits in the chair of the child and asks, "What happened in your childhood?" Then the client switches chairs and plays the part of the parent and provides an empathetic response. Careful facilitation of this exercise has brought floods of tears and such huge healings. It's amazing how pain can be transformed and healing insights come.

Dive a little deeper to the fear of being *abandoned* by someone who is supposed to love you! Long-held deep secrets around abuse often lead to extreme jealousy and mistrust in later intimate relationships.

I believe the root of my mother's jealousy, and the reason she became such a bitter woman, was that her own mother knew her daughter was being abused and did nothing. My mother's mother was so terrified to tell anyone, and she died young from breast cancer. I am sure her mother's guilt for not putting a stop to what she knew was going on between her daughter and her husband contributed to her cancer. (From listening to many women's abuse stories—and sometimes those of men—I learned that the mother or someone in the family often knows about the abuse, yet stays in denial!)

This scenario is played out in so many ways. It comes down to being abandoned by those who are supposed to love you. If, as you read this, you are aware of always feeling abandoned, I suggest seeing an experienced counselor, because there are so many good ways of healing that nightmare! Family therapist Virginia Satir works with a therapeutic method known as Family Constellation; it is a wonderful and insightful way of working things out as a family. Plus, I recommend the rebirthing work of Sondra Ray. In her book *Pele's Wish: Secrets of the Hawaiian Masters and Eternal Life*, she lists spiritual writer Leonard Orr's "Five Biggies in Life":

1. The birth trauma
2. The parental disapproval syndrome

3. Specific negatives
4. The unconscious death urge
5. Other lifetime work

Limiting beliefs in our culture can create divorce and separation

I know I still love my present partner, yet our lack of alternative models of intimacy, and the limiting beliefs we have been "domesticated" by, tell us that "open relationships" can be too difficult. I realize I need to be careful with whom I share my beliefs with, because society's limiting beliefs about sexuality and open relationships can be so full of assumptions and pain around the subject.

Let me say that I never regret attracting my present partner. I take full responsibility for my lack of awareness and consciousness about being (possibly) a natural polyamorist. I don't want to hide; I want to be real. How about *you*?

Choose beliefs that support you, including beliefs about God

Here is a very important suggestion from Louise Hay: *"Get a concept of God that supports you!"*

I love this thought. My religious upbringing did give me one benefit—it got me out of the house on Sundays, for peace. My parents came once to church; they thought it would be good for us children to go to church and have a religious education!

My spiritual journey has, at times, been very disciplined. And then it waned, as I felt there was always basic criticism and fear at the heart of religion. In my opinion, fear-based religion develops from the reaction of souls who have not learned to love themselves! (That could start a conversation!) I could not cope with feelings of being so wrong and guilt-ridden when I came out of church services.

As a counselor, I listened to so many stories of adults having been sexually or spiritually abused in so-called religious families as children.

I could not match what Jesus said with what came out of the mouths of "often angry pulpit priests" (whose own childhood was very suspect) and what truly was going on in reality. The Roman Catholic Church is facing a deep truth about the celibacy of their priests leading to sexual and emotional abuse. Please hear me: I am not against religion; yet I do feel each of us is naturally highly spiritual, and we don't need an "expert" middleman or woman. Enough said.

Insight: Gratitude is very healing. Giving thanks frequently gives me spiritual awakening and real joy. I love to wake up giving thanks for my breath, my body, my family, my bed. Now I can authentically be full of gratitude for my parents! Wow, that feels so good! What could you give thanks for? So much more joy and love will come your way if you are grateful for what you have. I even give thanks for those who judge me harshly about being open to loving more than one woman. Here's a little Persian story that says a lot about experts and ego:

The Sailor and the Teacher

Ayra earned his living by taking people on short boat trips. He came from a nautical family, and although he'd never had any formal education, he had learned all about sailing from his father and grandfather.

One day a schoolteacher, who fancied a few hours at sea in order to rest from the rigors of the classroom, hired him. He'd not been on Ayra's boat long before he asked: "What do you think the weather's going to be like today, Ayra?"

The sailor assessed the strength of the wind, examined the sky, looked at the sea and then said, "I think we is going to have a storm."

The teacher looked shocked. "What? Can't you speak properly? You shouldn't say 'we is.' You should say 'we are'! Didn't anyone teach you grammar?"

"I'm a sailor," replied Ayra. "What do I need grammar for?"

"Because, if you don't know grammar, half your life is wasted!" the teacher sneered, as he settled down to read his

book. Within minutes, and just as Ayra had predicted, the storm clouds began to gather, and the waves became choppy. Ayra became anxious as the boat was tossed on the rough sea.

"*Did you ever learn to swim?*" *asked Ayra.*

"*Why should I learn to swim? I'm a schoolteacher!*"

"*Well then your whole life is wasted, because this boat is going to sink any minute now!*

Here's another little story about the arrogance of assumptions:

The Ship and the Lighthouse

The ship's captain, seeing what appears to be another boat coming towards him, radios: "Unidentified vessel, you are on a trajectory that is going to collide with us. I suggest you move.

The reply: "Captain of the ship approaching, I suggest you change your course."

Captain of the ship: "I'll have you know I am captain of a very large ship. I insist that you move."

Reply: You may be a big ship, but I'm a lighthouse—your call!"

School and first job

If you reflect on my history, as I have shared it here, you may be able to see why I had little trust in adults, which was confirmed by my dear head teacher at secondary school, who said, in front of the whole school on my last day (I don't want to write this; it still makes me ashamed), "King, you are a waste of space!" And he added, rather vindictively in a deep baritone Welsh accent (nothing against him being Welsh), "You will make nothing of yourself." That humiliation in front of the whole school made me so angry. I thought very slowly, *I will show you, mate!* I had come into school labeled as a "dunce"; now I was leaving labeled as a "waste of space." ("*Perhaps, Roger, that challenge inspired you towards the wonderful being you became.*"—*Chelle*) Thank you, my dear friend Chelle!

I could not get out of school quick enough. I left with one O level in technical drawing and a whole lot of raw emotional hatred stored inside me. This reminds me of another little story:

The Mouse and the Bull

A mouse bit a bull on the nose, and the bull, enraged by such impudence, chased after it. The tiny mouse disappeared into a hole in a wall, so the bull charged against the wall bashing it again and again with his horns until he was quite worn out. He sank to the ground for a rest, whereupon the cheeky mouse came out and bit him again! The bull got to his feet, determined to catch his tormentor this time, but the mouse disappeared once more into the hole, leaving the bull with nothing to do but snort and bellow in hopeless anger. Soon he heard a little voice from inside the wall: "You big brutes don't always get your own way; sometimes we little ones get the better of you."

This shadows the story of David and Goliath, and the story Cinderella, as well as other fairy stories that tell of those who are small of stature overcoming the giants. So often I listen to true stories of abuse, and yet what is so amazing is that the pain can be alchemized into wise healing with real love and forgiveness.

DIVE
5

Meeting my first real teacher and positive role model

A Buddhist proverb: "When the student is ready the teacher appears!"
And I add, "in strange places!"

One of the turning points in my life occurred when I was fifteen. I
left school in deep pain, and a few days later got on a train to London
from Reading, the town nearest to my hometown. I cannot remember
what drove me to do this; I just knew in my heart I could not take any
more violence from my "crazy" family members. My sisters had left
home by this time; one was at university, and the other had married.

In my steam train compartment (one of the last I was on) sat a very
bright-eyed, grey-haired man wearing wire spectacles. Straight out he
asked me, "What are you going to do with your life, son?" I remember
looking around to see if there was an invisible person in this otherwise
empty carriage. I realized he was talking to me. That showed me how
low my personal esteem was ... nobody had ever asked such a gentle
question to me with a genuine concern.

Shocked, I stuttered, "I—I have no idea." He smiled and said, "I
invite you to come and see me in the East End of London. I may have
something interesting for you to do with your life."

Somehow, for once, I trusted a stranger—this man. Looking back,
I recognize this "chance" meeting as a miracle sent in disguise. I could
have so easily ended up homeless in London and gone into total despair.
Indeed, many victims of low self-esteem, especially young people, go
into cities searching for themselves as I did. Many of them get sucked

into prostitution and drugs if their thoughts remain negative and they find no opportunities for advancement. I would love to imagine and be part of a movement that radiates in every family, community, society and country: If you change your thoughts you change your life!

This man turned out to be Sir Alec Dickson, who helped start the charity, Oxfam! Well, I went to the address and was interviewed for the post of community volunteer. This led to my working for a year and a half with the mentally handicapped, and then with mentally ill people. I loved this work. For once in my life, I had a defined role, and in a strange way I felt I belonged. It is such an important need in us all: *a need to belong* to something that's hopefully worthwhile!

Insight: Today I connect with people, both young and old, who want to join and belong to alternative communities with values that are truly mindful of our ecological and human precariousness; my partner and my daughter are so keen on this, and I support them.

What amazed me out of this work of caring, cooking, cleaning, and listening to hurt people was that I actually found deep satisfaction. The wardens of both hostels I worked in believed in me and showed it by giving me good references.

Then Alec interviewed me for the toughest job I think I have ever had. This was to help start and run the first "rehabilitation" hostel for ex-prisoners in Leeds, Yorkshire.

Turning my ability to "survive the family" into a skill and life-long work

I nervously took a train north; this was the first time I had traveled to what I thought was D.H. Lawrence country. (That was Nottingham). I had read *Sons and Lovers* at fourteen; and this book spoke to me about my own family. Later I read *Lady Chatterley's Lover*—a real blockbuster because it involved explicit sexual descriptions. I remember everybody talking excitedly about this bold and daring book. Lawrence certainly shifted consciousness about what sort of "secret life" went on behind "closed doors."

I was just sixteen years of age, tall and gangly, when I was interviewed by three probation officers in a courtroom. I stood literally in the dock! After asking me my motives for working with hardened criminals, I replied, "I am good at communicating with hurt people!" Who put that answer into my head I don't know! Possibly the divine.

They took me on. I don't think anyone else wanted the post; the previous volunteer had lasted only two weeks. So I was paid £1 and 10 shillings per week for a post for which I was so academically unqualified, yet for which my crazy family upbringing made me an ideal candidate. Well, I like to think that! A sixteen-year-old certainly would not be allowed to do this work today! I imagine the newspapers and trade unions would have a field day, plus all of the health and safety issues! This was all preparation for my becoming a student of raw life by working with very dark, hurt souls, particularly men.

The voluntary work was like a baptism by fire, though not much more dangerous than living within my own family. The work with ex-prisoners was at times hell, yet I had tremendous guile that became a gift. I learned to connect with people who were worse off than I was. I could somehow get through to them. Little shocked me—or so I made out. My present partner has often said, "You have a natural gift for running groups." True or not, I do feel some energy runs through me that allows me to trust the energy in the people and myself. Perhaps it's the power of *now*. My body is so alive and integrated with mind and spirit. The same happens when I give talks; I can take ages preparing them, the words may change, and it's as if divine wisdom inspires me. I give thanks for this gift and it is my intention to use it wisely to benefit others.

Protection

At the hostel, I learned how to work with groups and use the different personalities to offset conflict and violence. The probation officers were often scared to come into the hostel and would ask me to bring their clients out to their cars. I was so egotistically proud that I could mix with such colorful souls, who often told me their horrific stories, even though once or twice two men were so triggered by their memories of hurt that they threatened to kill me! But somehow there was a "presence" protecting me; I learned to talk them down. For once in my life I felt strangely at home. The hardest part of the job was coping with the warden who was a tough ex-miner who had no empathy and little skill in communicating with the men. I do admit some of the men were not easy. They had murdered, robbed, abused people, and some were burnt-out ex-mental patients who were completely institutionalized.

Insight: I often see that the people who care for people in institutions of despair are as hurt or even more damaged than the people they care for. Consequently, instances of staff members abusing inmates appear on the news. We need a way of truly caring for the care givers. These include prison wardens, teachers, police officers, doctors, social workers, nurses, and many others. (As an aside, recent research on men in prison showed that one in four men is dyslexic).

Robert Holden, founder and director of The Happiness Project and Success Intelligence, has written a book called *Loveability: Knowing How to Love and Be Loved.* I quote from his first chapter: *"One Day, all the great professions will include love in their training syllabi and core values."*

Dr. Ihaleakala Hew Len teaches workshops on the Hawaiian method for achieving wealth, health, peace, and happiness, and teaches Ho'oponopono, an ancient Hawaiian practice of reconciliation and forgiveness. This mantra is an integral part of Ho'oponopono: *"I love you. I'm sorry. Please forgive me. Thank you."*

Each morning at the hostel, I would find women and/or men in bed with each other. The smell of alcohol was everywhere, and I would find broken furniture after fights. I learned to take this all in my stride. I remember being addicted, as were all the inmates, to smoking at sixteen years of age. It was a way of sharing even if it was killing us!

The police would often raid the place if there had been a local burglary. This created a lot of hatred and mistrust.

One particular incident happened while I was there: the Welsh Aberfan coal disaster. A landslide of coal slag killed many children and teachers. What amazed me were the tears in these so-called hardened men, who had been so condemned by society and unloved. This disaster led to deep sharing amongst the men and changed many attitudes and behavior in the hostel. From then on there was an honor amongst thieves! We cooperated and assisted each other, from laying the tables for meals to admitting wrongdoings, like theft. Out of tough experiences good can come. I witnessed a lot of healing at 56 Morris Lane, Leeds. I left this voluntary job after a year, a very different young man, yet still I had many unresolved emotional issues.

Going back home

After a year and a half, I went back home, only to find my father one day in bed with his mistress at their place of work—a sports shop. So I went and told my mother to come and live with me in a rented cottage with my two West Indian friends. This is where I let my mother have her "break open" (as opposed to a "breakdown") because she was so distraught. It was six months before she could stop crying and was able to have a coherent conversation. I did not want her to go back into the "psychiatrist's chair" and be given ECT and drugs.

Choosing to live my life

The big turning point came when my father turned up saying, "I want my wife back, but would you come and live with us, because you understand us both?" I was angry and dumbfounded. I had a place at university; I had got my exams at night school. For the first time in my life I said, "No!" I stood up to my father and said very calmly: "You need to look after my mother by letting her set up home where she wants." (I love, in my Heal Your Life sessions, getting people to say. "No! No! No! No!" And really shout it out. Once, in our room, which was next door to the Women's Institute meeting, I got a man saying "No!" He increased his anger and shouted, "F**k off, Mother!" Then, we just burst out laughing, as there was complete silence from next door. I hope there were not too many mothers next door who felt they deserved that comment.)

My mother taking her power was a big turning point for me. I assisted my parents to part on reasonably friendly terms.

Insight: I have had clients who have given up their dreams by not living their own life and letting the demands of others' outweigh their own true needs, possibly living with them 'til they had no time left to create their true purpose. Well, I was not going to do this; I had learned I could take my power back. As professional counselor John Bradshaw says in his excellent book *Homecoming: Reclaiming and Championing Your Inner Child*: *"Heal your wounded inner child"*

Well, I took my power back, and so did my mother. She went to Bournemouth and started to live with some joy. I went to university at Bradford, Yorkshire.

University and its limitations

I got my exams by attending night school after being inspired by a man called Gary Turner, who believed in me enough that I could study and go to college.

I went to college and studied psychology, sociology, and history, yet found little inspiration. Nobody mentioned metaphysics or why or how to love yourself. It was all about rats and statistics. It was about memory and cramming knowledge. So college gave me very few clues as to who I was or what my purpose could be. I just got through by becoming a rebel. I was easily spotted as a potential left-wing student who had a lot of anger. I realize now, organized religion and political parties thrive on people like who I was then. I have counseled young angry men who could have easily joined a terrorist brigade. I was lucky I had one professor who recognized I was gifted. He wanted me to go to Oxford and do a masters degree. I turned it down out of fear and Marxist indoctrination. Oh well!

As I type this, the thoughts make my tummy churn. I feel open to your gaze. Yet somewhere, I need to let you know where this human came from, and it does not excuse my mistakes later in life. Over the years, I have done lots of therapy on myself. I have joined men's groups and sat in them, listening and sometimes sharing; yet I have never been able to say who I truly am or how I am truly feeling. I don't think polyamory was ever talked about. Men often talked about "affairs," yet their discussions always implied secrecy and lies.

Second teacher: death and grief and a new process of beginning

I am going to jump now, to when I was in my second marriage, ten years after my university days. I had just returned from a holiday in Cyprus, and I had a call early that morning in which I learned that my close friend, Alec, had died aged sixty-five from a heart attack. That's my age now!

The shock was immense. I went to his funeral the next day, and during the song: "The First Time Ever I Saw Your Face," written by Ewan MacColl and sung by Roberta Flack, I burst out crying and could not stop. I was not only crying for losing Alec; I was crying for his life ending—and I was crying for myself. He had been a kind man… a big man, whom I trusted. He was one of the few friends I had let close to me in my life. He had taught me to windsurf and given me pleasure and joy and surrogate fathering. I was so distraught I could hardly do anything.

Have you ever had a shock that suddenly caused everything to overwhelm you? My grieving over his death brought forth all the hurt emotional patterns of loss from my childhood and teenage years. All the "father-type love" I had ever experienced was gone. I was inconsolable.

Insight: If you ask a man to talk safely about his relationship with his father, a child's tears usually erupt.

A tape that gave me good information

Then a special divine accident happened. I was so desperate for something to help me that I went to the local library and wandered around and found a tape section, and in that section was Louise Hay's

You Can Heal Your Life. It just picked me … and I put it in my car tape player and started to drive. I didn't know where I was going, yet I listened over and over again to the information on the four little tapes. The tears came more and more. The pain surfaced, and for a month I didn't listen to any news—just Louise's voice informing me that I could love *me* and heal my hurts with love and forgiveness. (I went to bed listening to her, night after night!)

And if you have read her books, you probably have had your own unique experiences. As an aside, I had learned about the book many years earlier; however, I had not been open to the wisdom then. It took a dear friend's death and then my defenses coming to the surface for me to look and learn. The loss of a gentle surrogate father was to be a big turning point for my healing.

That started a whole series of lessons, and I loved the journey inward (most of the time). I was exploring a lost child. I read book after book, like *Self Parenting: The Complete Guide to Your Inner Conversations* by John K. Pollard III. This boy, teenager, parent, adult—this human being called Roger—was going to love every emotional age in him and take his power back. I wanted to contact my inner "genius child" who could be re-parented with love and forgiveness.

Consequently, the *Universe* brought me books and tapes, each one coming to me exactly at the right time. I wanted to re-parent myself and be the person I knew deep down I was. I set myself little targets: saying positive affirmations. I wrote them down and put them everywhere. I knew I now had one of the habits that Stephen Covey explained in his book: *The 7 Habits of Highly Effective People: Powerful Lessons in Personal Change.*

I had good knowledge coupled with learning and practicing, and later teaching, these new skills of self love, combined with a deep desire, or willpower, to change my life for the better. So a "paradigm shift" happened, and is still going on. I began to write my first book: *Love The Miracle You Are.* All the books are sold out. I have recorded myself reading the book on my website www.rogerking.info, which is managed by a wise man, Richard Gentle, who has written many interesting books—some of which you'll find listed in the appendix.

Love The Miracle You Are

I found myself writing this book every morning. I self-published it and wrote a few more books, because I needed to be creative with what I was learning about *me*. I am sure some people thought I had gone a bit crazy. However, I carried on learning and bringing my knowledge into my counseling practice and group work. Clients thrived, despite their subconscious resistance to loving themselves. This taught me patience. I have one client who has come nearly every week for ten years. He smiled one day and said, "I must test your patience." I replied, "Yes, and it's a good lesson for me too. Thank you." He may come to the next series of Heal Your Life… Wow, what a miracle!

I felt that the institution of the "church" judged me harshly. So my partner and I left what we felt was becoming hypocritical. Then, three years ago, I had enough money and chose to become a qualified and licensed Heal Your Life facilitator. I was trained by a lovely woman, Patricia Crane. That course confirmed what I already knew in my soul: I was ready for change, and it took time for the transition to occur.

This reminds me of one of many sayings of Lao-Tse, a philosopher in ancient China:

> *Life is a series of natural and spontaneous changes.*
> *Don't resist them—that only creates sorrow.*
> *Let things flow naturally forward*
> *In whatever way they like.*

Insight: The more I love *me* with all of my imperfections and mistakes, the more creative I become. Out of the sorrow of parting from my partner is coming true joy. We truly want the best for each other.

DIVE

6

Everything in my experience, especially in relationships, is a mirror of the mental pattern that is going on inside me! When I lie to myself, it hurts and creates more lies. Until I confront those half-truths and come clean, I hide my true talents, and my ego stops my ability to love life.

—*Roger*

I now run Heal Your Life sessions weekly. They are so rich in their search for authentic and courageous ways to allow our lives to become more open and honest without judgment. I feel such a sense of purpose when I see people come into the room, full of their negative beliefs about life and especially themselves. And then we start and move step by step to teach and listen and share. Through each session, I vision and witness people's mental and spiritual hearts expanding with forgiveness and truly owning their family emotional patterns that have hindered awareness of the inner miracle of their lives. To hide our miracle of love is such a waste of energy. The music of their souls shines great healing to each other. As trust grows, I do less teaching and let their "heart wisdom" begin to open new doors of opportunity. I just give thanks for the process that unravels each person's unique healing. Sometimes I am asked, "What is good health?" Then I remember, word for word, the following quote from *Heart Thoughts*, by Louise Hay:

Good health
Is having no fatigue,
Having a good appetite,
Going to sleep and awakening easily,
Having a good memory.
Having good humor
Having precision in thought and action,
and being honest, humble, grateful and loving.
How healthy are you?

Well, I still have work to do; the real difference now is that I enjoy the journey even when it gets tough! Perhaps the title of my next book will be *Divine Mind Willing*.

DIVE

7

Healing through lovely music and dance

Men, we can heal! We just must stop lying to ourselves and blaming others. We can do it! We can dig deep with our love of truth and our vulnerability—then magic can happen. I would add, let go of being in control; let your ecstasy rip through your soul!

As I write, the DJ part of me gets inspiration from music. Now I am listening to "Moonshadow" by Cat Stevens. He sings with such meaning:

> *Yes, I'm being followed by a moonshadow*
> *Moonshadow, moonshadow*
> *Leaping and hopping on a moonshadow*
> *Moonshadow, moonshadow*

And later:

> *Yes, if I ever lose my mouth*
> *Oh, if… I won't have to talk…*

I never realized that my words created my reality until I learned to study metaphysics and all of the self-help books that I would love to have been taught at school and college. My shadow of the past has followed me, and I have often wallowed in it. I have driven my life looking in the mirror of the past. Not wise staying there. Just take forgiveness and kindness there and the Divine will give such gifts of insight and healing. This may seem a bit clumsy, I know; yet it's like a soft breeze on a cloudless day bathing every part of your mind, body, and spirit.

Imagine driving your car, looking in the rearview mirror. I did that for a long time! Now I imagine going through a holy fire that's revealing every aspect of life and healing our spirits for the next adventure.

"Will it take long to find *me*?" You may ask. Well I have taken sixty-five years to find *me*. I suggest you don't wait so long to learn who you are! You and I have got work to do. There are people we can touch with our love and healing. I sense that, if you have picked up this book and not condemned me, we have met on the checkerboard of life.

Suggestion: Never become a go-between! I always wonder: *Why is it that family members sometimes treat each other worse than they treat anyone else they know?* Usually, people are *angry* and don't know it, yet they take it out on everyone who tries to get close. I suggest: Never be a go-between, especially between souls who are hurting! Having to listen to two people—my parents—talk about each other with such anger often frightened me and exhausted me mentally and emotionally. The one strong decision I did make as an adult was to keep my wife and children away from my original family. This I am proud of, yet it makes me sad. I knew intuitively that I had to do it. I am sure many who read this have done the same with their own families.

I see how my painful past has been under the surface of all my major decisions. In both of my main relationships I was still influenced by my inner wounded child, feeling a sense of loneliness and disconnection. I had little true center. And I realize my fear of truth came from covering up the fact that I did not feel "good enough."

What I feared I then attracted

Of course that is what I attracted in my early love life—women who were angry and/or did not feel good about themselves, usually from having been badly abused. I ended one such relationship when a woman I had broken up with started following me. I believed she might come into my house and kill me for leaving. It's called being stalked. I have always remembered that her love was so possessive. Towards the end of our relationship I felt like a piece of meat. There was no love or warmth. I do feel now that I am not putting that vibration out to women, so no women stalk me.

I stopped looking for love outside *me*

Let me say more about my wife and me. We were strongly attracted to one another when we met at a party. I had gate-crashed with a friend, and when my wife and I first saw each other, we felt a strong connection. Before meeting her, I had made a promise to have a break from intimate relationships. I wanted to stop looking for love from somebody else. I just wanted friends. I wanted to know more about who I truly was.

Then it was like one hour later, the *Universe* said: "Okay, you're being honest, and so I give you your next partner." I am so glad that I met my second partner. I dreamed her, and she dreamed me!

After the romantic phase of our relationship, we had our early storms, and then *we* got pregnant with our beautiful Shelley. I was still so frightened of commitment after one failed marriage. I was so pleased that we could share with integrity.

What a wonderful relationship we had. We could talk and share and, while the children were at home, my faith was steady and happy. It was such a relief to be with a soul who did not condemn me for being the way I was. We never discussed "polyamory" or "open marriage" in the early years; it was not in our awareness. We were both committed to personal growth (and still are). When we got married, my partner wanted me to be sexually faithful to her. I felt this was what I wanted too.

We both had emotional hurts from the past that, when triggered, were tough to work through. Then we brought Simon, our son, into the world, and we learned to parent with real love as best we could. My wife gave up any career in the first years of our children's lives. She is a very loving mother, and our children love her deeply. I want to add that they love me, as well. I know I love all my children deeply. All our grown up children get along well together, and that is such a blessing.

A big love!

My present partner and I loved each other, although our energies were always very different. We rarely saw eye to eye on personal philosophy and when I trained to become a licensed Heal Your Life workshop leader and life coach, my new insights somehow exaggerated our differences. I realized that, the more I wanted my partner to see life through my reality, the less we had true joy! We both needed space and time to re-find our wholehearted joy for living and continued friendship.

I love my wife and always will. I truly want what is best for her as well as for myself. We are talking as I write this book, and I know that, with divine guidance, she is finding her strength and directing it into her amazing creative genius. Her art is everywhere in our beautiful little house. Now it is time to let go and move on.

One huge lesson I am learning is that, as I learn to love myself from a place of truth and respect, no matter what challenges I face, "good" will come out of it.

Insight: The more I stopped looking for love outside *me* and loved myself just as I am, with deep truth and respect, the happier I became. Also, gradually, I became more open and receptive to love from others. I continue to love my partner unconditionally and honor her unique journey.

Taking full responsibility and letting go

I hope this little book can help you let go of the secrets you have chosen to hold, and learn that loving *you* is such a gift from a deep spiritual place inside your mind and body. You can reverse your reasons for delaying to love *you* and life, and learn to treat yourself and others in a type of holy relationship. Once I accepted full responsibility for everything in my life, it seemed much more difficult to judge another person.

The definition for "holy relationship" comes from *A Course in Miracles* (forgive the masculine!):

> *Each one has looked within and seen no lack. Accepting his completion, he would extend it by joining with another; whole as himself... This relationship has heaven's holiness. Think of what a holy relationship can teach!"* Whereas, an unholy relationship is based on differences, where each one thinks the other has what he has not. They come together, each to complete himself and rob the other. They stay until they think there is nothing left to steal, and then they move on. And so they wander through the world, strangers.

Dancing has become part of my daily healing practice. This goes deep into the body. (I have just taken a break from writing ... and spent it dancing on the veranda to great soul music: "The Ecstasy of Dancing Fleas" by Virgil Pink, performed by the Penguin Cafe Orchestra.

If you disagree with everything I have said...

What can you do to me, a sixty-five-year-old man?" Can you imprison me for being who I am? This book is not just about confession; it's about dissolving all the hooks and threats that our double-standard society puts on us; that each of us helped to make!

I now want to come from the angle that, when I am truthful with a caring, loving intention, I can truly connect to my divine intention and to that similar, yet unique, part in *you*, which has learned to keep so many secrets that hurt you in your mind, body, and soul. This may be an assumption. Are you squeaky clean?

Looking out from this mountain villa, I see a deep blue sky. There are no clouds of guilt, resentment, or fear. What blocks love and forgiveness is constant *criticism*. In addition, the cloudy thunderous thoughts of self-criticism gradually kill the ability of the soul to receive from Spirit. My own self-criticism so often comes from my belief in my guilt. Don Miguel explains in his book, *The Four Agreements: A Practical Guide to Personal Freedom* that humans have long memories and will chastise themselves a thousand times—or others will do so. In the animal kingdom, a mistake is acknowledged and addressed only once by both the offender and his or her companions. Would it not be healthier in our society to stop making ourselves so full of fear and just love whom we are?

I have seen people come out of places of despair, like churches and mosques, looking so beaten down with fear for being human. I know there is a loving *being* that must cry at how we have conditioned ourselves to create so much violence inside and outside in our world, all in the name of what *appears* to be spiritual. I want to cry from my heart: "Please let us stop saying and believing, 'My god is better than your god'!" This comes from such wounded conditioning and consciousness. I realize I never want to be perfect! I am *me*, and that includes both my tough and my loveable parts. This combination makes me human and spiritually more aware and connected to life. A little story: *A tramp knocks at the door of a church, and no one will let him in. Suddenly, a voice echoes from above (God). "Don't bother! I've been trying to get in there for ages!"*

Be your "self"

Many of us feel we live in a society that often wants to control us and make us think the same as everyone else, so that we "fit in". Yet my spirit is unique, just as yours is unique. Here's a fitting story by Leo Buscaglia called Educated Insolence:

> *The animals got together in the forest one day and decided to start a school. There was a rabbit, a bird, a squirrel, a fish, and an eel, and they formed a Board of Education. The rabbit insisted that running be in the curriculum. The bird insisted that flying be in the curriculum. The fish insisted that swimming be in the curriculum, and the squirrel insisted that perpendicular tree climbing be in the curriculum. They put all of these things together and wrote a Curriculum Guide.*

Then they insisted that all of the animals take all of the subjects. Although the rabbit was getting A in running, perpendicular tree climbing was a real problem for him; he kept falling over backwards. Pretty soon he got to be brain damaged and he couldn't run any more. He found that instead of making an A in running he was making a C, and of course he always made an F in perpendicular tree climbing.

The bird was really beautiful at flying, but when it came to burrowing in the ground, he couldn't do so well. He kept breaking his beak and wings. Pretty soon he was making a C at flying as well as an F in burrowing, and he had a bad time with perpendicular tree climbing.

The moral of the story is that the person who was best of the class was a mentally retarded eel who did everything in a halfway fashion. But the educators were all happy because everybody was taking all of the subjects and it was called broad-based education.

I invite you to respect the fact that we are all so different—valuing freedom to think in our own minds and able to *become a person with a unique talent* of being a miracle of *warrior* love! What blesses one blesses all! Happiness is sure to come from such creativity. If anyone wants you to conform, just send him or her love and go on along your very own path of loving life.

A little test

Recently, a man came up to me while I sat outside one of my favorite café's in Wakefield, UK. I was preparing a talk. He said, leaning close to me, "You think you know everything! You have got it all worked out." I had seen the Asian man before, but we had never conversed.

Then he got even more aggressive. "You are so smug and just so superior!" I asked, "Have I done anything to offend you?" He walked off and then suddenly came back and ranted again. I suddenly blessed him with love. And off he went.

Insight: I ask myself, *what is it within me that is creating this experience?* Was I in such a moment of doubt, vibrating a resonance that attracted his negativity?

The Universe sends us all kinds of tests; this one came just as I was preparing a talk on "positive attitudes" to a MIND group in Bradford. Sometimes people will despise your vibration of love, and their hurt leads to an inner envy. Remember; be aware as you change to be the unique expression of the divine mind in you. A series of experiences may come to test you. I love the biblical quote: *"He who does not love does not know God, for God is love."* 1 John 4:8

Love thy neighbor as thy self.

The thing is, we have forgotten why we should love ourselves, and we have forgotten how to love ourselves. If we are open to loving ourselves, we can love our neighbors and our God within. I was doing a talk on how to be real about loving *you* just as you are! At the halfway break, a well-dressed woman came up and said, "I have always thought of God as being out there on some cloud; now I realize the true God is in me. Thank you. I feel so real." I am always amazed and thankful that when I show up as honest as I can be, some healing takes place in the person or group I am facilitating. Once we get our egos out of the way, the Source works through us. Wayne Dyer, in his book, *The Shift: Taking Your Life from Ambition to Meaning*, reminds me:

"When I speak or write, I encounter opinions different from my own. I know that if I speak to a thousand people, there will be a thousand separate opinions of me in that audience."

And then he quotes Paramananda

"And do not imagine that anyone can have true faith in God who has not faith in himself."

83

And Wayne ends with what I can battle with:

> *"If I choose to give up faith in myself by listening to the entreaties of my ego, then I cannot have faith in my Source of being—they're always intertwined."*

DIVE

8

What secrets have you convinced yourself never to share?

Unexpressed anger that spills over into resentment eats away at our minds, bodies, and souls. And, moreover, it attracts other people's resentment, and then we all go down a black hole together being *right*—however, sick with dis-ease, or dead! To want to be right and not let our anger be released safely is not healthy for loving relationships, whether open or closed. So many people I listen to tell me deep secrets that they feel they must carry and they must never tell family, friends, or anyone. The inside of that person's body becomes like a private hell. This burden often makes them hypersensitive and often obsessive and extremely resentful. These "imperfections" prevent wholehearted living. The self has to hide, and there is no self-compassion.

I've learned that most of my clients came from religious families in which they were terrified by critical abuse spiritually, sexually, and/or emotionally to a point that they could not think in their own minds. I have spent over forty years with people, sharing, and this has been a gift of inspiration for me and, hopefully for those I have listened to. Often people come and want to just stay angry, which reminds me of my next story. The law of attraction certainly works in mysterious ways. Well, if my karma is to pay off some tough stuff

I did in past lives, I truly believe I have done that by being around some angry souls.

Apple Pie and Ice Cream

> *A passenger on a train was giving his order to the waiter: "For desert, I'll have apple pie and ice cream."*
>
> *"Sorry, sir, we don't have any left. Would you choose something else?"*
>
> *The passenger was fuming with anger. "What!" he shouted. "How is it possible that you don't have such a simple thing as apple pie? What an incompetent shower! I'll have you know that I am a friend of the managing director of this railway, and he will surely hear about this. In fact, I'll call him immediately!"*
>
> *As the man searched for his phone, the chef, who had overheard the commotion, called the waiter over. "We'll be able to get apple pie at the next stop in a few minutes. There's no problem."*
>
> *Sure enough, an apple pie was procured, and the waiter brought it, with a big blob of ice cream, to the irate passenger, who was still letting everyone know of his disgust. "Here you are, sir. Apple pie and ice cream with the compliments of the chef and a complimentary brandy."*
>
> *The man banged his fist on the table.*
>
> *"Take it away ... and the brandy! I'd much rather be angry!"*

This was from Anthony de Mello; no pleasing some people.

Fire walks became a time for change!

Do we live in a dungeon of past hurt and fear of future, or a palace of possibility?

When I did my first fire walk, it blew my mind that we could choose to walk on red-hot coals without getting burnt. What scientists say is impossible. Well, we can do it with our mind, body, and spirit, in total harmony. My Chi was higher than the fire's Chi!

"*I am limitless*" was my affirmation as I walked across those red coals on a wet night. It was like calling my spirit back. And out of that fire walk came this new affirmation:

> "*I surround myself with people I love and they love me and we have honest and true friendship!*"

I know the two fire walks I did, gave me a massive inner courage, to know whatever comes down the tube of life I can handle it with less lies and self-deception. If I can walk on hot coals and not burn, I can face truth and change myself for the better, without crucifying myself and making myself so wrong. It felt like a process of purification.

I realized I was taught to be angry and lie by my original family to survive. Somewhere at that fire walk I choose to be honest, even if those choices hurt those I love. I could hide no longer for fear of hurting those close to me. It took time for me to be honest to my partner and I regret that delay with all my heart.

I do encourage you to join a well-run fire walk. Patrick MacManaway was a wise and worthy facilitator. The fire walks became like a holy fire burning off my lies to myself. One of the many outcomes of the fire walks is a decision to do less counseling and choosing to be with people I truly feel reflect my honesty of who I have become. I love facilitating *growth* groups because, as I have said earlier, the people are prepared to take good risks to be real!

Resistance to loving self

This is my opinion:

> *"Deep recurring resistance to loving ourselves often originates from either oppressive overprotection by parents, or not being protected at all in early childhood. The link between these two opposites is we consistently doubt who we are. We cannot just be and be enough! We live life in the pain of the past and fear of the future."* You are free to disagree.

Either of these emotional patterns at each end of the physical and emotional continuum can lead a soul to be deeply angry, resentful and resistant to becoming free in learning to love self and be true to self and others. Doubt of self is a kind of inner crime we do to ourselves. I see so-called righteous anger can be used to get us out of bad relationships and it can [without awareness] lead us into worse relationships, with even more anger!

I was not protected in childhood; I had to fight for nearly everything. The big consequence was, I doubted life except for my physicality; my energy. I relied on force to give me what I thought I wanted. The consequence of that was not to let love in or out; I just hid behind many masks. I wanted to control everything and everybody by seeking continual approval or, if I couldn't get what I needed, I would slip into an unconscious pattern of criticizing others. I never found peace or self-acceptance, until I realized it was all right to learn how to love me. This *me* was desperate to find love.

The fire walks and continually learning to love the real me, all parts of me, became a big turning point. I had to become more honest even if that meant losing everybody including my family and all who thought they knew me. I had to *come out* and *come home* to my more real self.

In my opinion children whose personal power was overprotected (or dominated) by patriarchy or severe matriarchy can grow up doubting their own self-worth. And in extreme over-protection we can lose any real sense of self-worth and self-compassion. I love the affirmation:

> *"I go beyond the negative limitations of others and my own with increasing self-love and self-compassion."*

Different realities

We each have unique lessons. I certainly don't choose to learn your lessons for you or expect you to learn mine. There are so many different realities for us all; we cannot see reality in the same way. Yet, like the stars, we are all connected in a constellation and somehow we affect each other—especially if it's true that our thought joins to others' thought. If we hate and harbor resentment, then those are the same thoughts that will return in our day-to-day experiences.

So often, when anger is stored in the mind, body, and soul, we can be *unreachable* for a long time. I remember waking in the morning feeling wrong and full of aches and pains. However, I didn't listen to my body and what it was trying to tell me! A great way to wake up now is using affirmations that positively charge and change my energy. It's like experiencing the scent of a rose in the morning instead of continually *breaking wind* and being so morbid! When I was young, nobody asked me; "what would you like to do in life or be?" I was just controlled without any personal choice.

Now I enjoy saying to the mirror: *"What can I do, Roger, to make you happy today?"* And then I sing my affirmations as I shower. When I am "down", I remember the affirmation: "My thoughts are my best friends!"

As I freewheel down the mountain to the inviting sea, I remember what a gift life is, even in the searing heat. When I am cycling up and it gets tough, I put my iPod on and listen to a lecture, like *Embracing Change*, by Louise Hay. Then I am at the top of the climb and my mind and body have worked together so well. This may sound simplistic, yet it does work, I promise you. Men especially, I ask you to love yourselves and take good risks. Begin to face and share your truth. A little Buddhist story about the poverty of envy and comparing ourselves negatively:

The Rose and the Oak Tree

> An oak tree had been growing in the garden for over half a century, and it had been pretty happy with its situation. But when a nearby rose began to bloom in the summer, the oak tree became jealous. "Look at that lovely rose," the oak tree said. "The dew glistens on its beautiful pink petals, and everyone who passes it admires it. But look at me. I'm just the usual dirty brown color, with a few green leaves. How I wish I could be like that beautiful rose, so that people wouldn't ignore me!"
>
> The rose heard the oak tree's wish. It had been secretly impressed by the tree's great height and strength. "I'll change places with you for a day if you like," said the rose. "Let's ask the garden spirits if they can arrange it."

The garden spirits were only too pleased to help. And the rose and oak tree changed places. Each of them was delighted with their appearances.

Later that day, though, the gardener came out and cut the rose to decorate for dinner!

There is a balance between expressing anger safely and not letting it rule your life! I have worked with clients who have been so angry and jealous, that they just kept creating relationships that hurt them. Nobody wanted to go near these people. So many bodily dis-eases are caused by the mind continually feeling: *I am not good enough. I should have been a much better person!* I implore you to let go of anger, guilt, criticism, and fear. They are so toxic. Find safe places to let it go. And find the root emotional weed (that is probably in thoughts and feelings that are results of a childhood trauma) and let it go forever. *Homecoming: Reclaiming and Championing Your Inner Child* by John Bradshaw, is a wonderful book to read and work through; I have known many people change dramatically after doing the exercises in this one book.

Insight from Wayne Dyer: "*Every fall has within it the potential to move us to a higher place. It may be necessary to get down and dirty in the dark of the night of the soul in order to free ourselves from the grip of the well-established ego.*"

Wayne Dyer points out Rumi's "tough love" observation:

"*The spiritual path wrecks the body and afterwards restores it to complete health. It destroys the house to unearth the treasure and with that treasure builds it better than before.*" From Rumi "Daylight."

The Power of thought

When we think or talk, I know I connect to similar people's thoughts. I affirm that: "My partner and I will let go of blame and let each other go with love and authentic forgiveness and rejoice in each other's newly found abundant joy. We will find our own wisdom, peace, and joy. Let us be so grateful that we were brought together for a particular space of time! And so it is."

What are you listening for in your life? This reminds me of a contemporary story:

The Cat and the Coins

Two friends, Ann and Mary, were out shopping in the city center one busy Saturday afternoon. The roads were full of traffic, and the noise of the engines revving, horns beeping, and stereos blasting joined the crying of children and the shouting of adults to produce a veritable cacophony.

Suddenly, Mary stopped and grabbed her friend by the arm. "Listen," she said, "I can hear a cat mewing. It seems to be in some distress."

"I can't hear anything," replied her friend. "Are you sure?"

"I'm sure I can hear it," said Mary. "Come on, I'll show you."

The two friends walked to a little grassy area by the side of the road, and there, hidden beneath a bush, was a little kitten in a brown cardboard box. Some cruel person must have left it there to die. Mary picked it up and stroked it tenderly. "You're coming home with me," she said.

"How on earth did you hear such a small sound in the middle of all this noise? You must have terrific hearing!" said Ann.

"No I haven't," said Mary, smiling. "It's no different from yours. Watch this." With that, she led her friend back on to the busy street, took a handful of change out of her bag, and scattered it onto the pavement. Every person within twenty yards turned round. "See," said Mary, "it all depends on what you're listening for!"

What are you listening for? Are you listening for experiences that will harbor your hurt and pain? Or can you be "willing" to change your thinking (emotional patterns) and love *you* a little more each day?

As I write this, a digital music service called Spotify on my laptop is playing my music collection. I'm now listening to Canadian musician and singer-songwriter, Son of Dave, sing "I am a Lover Not a Fighter."

That is a lovely affirmation that partially describes me. I do believe that, at times, I have been a fighter, yet I have always believed there must be more than what I have learned or been told. As I dance outside and feel the sun, I am coming to the end of the first eight dives into my soul and heart. I thank you for reading this far. I hope you will come with me as I get the inspiration.

DIVE
9

Expanding Heart of Love

My Louise Hay wisdom card today is: *"I express my true being today. This is a new day. I begin anew to claim and create all good in me that is good."*

One of my favorite songs is a tango that was brought to me by a lovely tango dance teacher at the Gaia Tribe's festival in Yorkshire. It's "We Love Love" by Carmel McCreagh. I thought this track could be the title of a book!

The song catches my spirit:

> *"Love falls, like a blanket over my head; Love falls; a feather unto my bed. Love falls, but I catch it before it lands. For love when it's lovely let's talk in circles that go either way; let's walk around the things we don't know how to say!*

Love of self clears the windows of our minds

Learning to love is like creating a new window in our own minds, where we experience something deeply spiritual.

We are souls who carry the eternal light. We carry the future within. Strength emanates from our souls, and we believe the more truthful and vulnerable we become, the more we touch others for good instead of leaving people feeling sorry for us. It is such a miraculous process to witness this real strength in ourselves in self-help groups where we talk of how to love ourselves. This is what this book is about, and hopefully my heart and soul journey can serve you.

I follow in many teachers' footsteps, yet I want to be the authentic me. I want my meaning and purpose to go out to the heart of your mind—that mind with which you truly choose what to think and say! I know the ego plays tricks, yet I have worried so much about that "parasite", it keeps me stuck on just painful memories.

To love "love" of self and life is such a gift. It's like picking up my beautiful five-month-old grandson and smiling into eyes of trusting divine love, and then having it returned multiplied from such innocence.

Just picked up *A Guide for the Advanced Soul: A Book of Insight* by Susan Hayward. As I hold the thought of my partner and I parting, this saying, which I see when I open the book, is so meaningful to me: *"Change is never a loss—it is change only."*—Vernon Edwards.

Vulnerability

When constant inner and outer criticism ceases, and love and acceptance is created, it is so much easier to be vulnerable and accept just how you are.

Here are my immediate thoughts and feelings on vulnerability:

- Just feeling like a six-year-old. Please look at me! I want to be noticed and loved just how I am!
- Being as truthful as I can be about being *me* in all situations that I have attracted to me and am responsible for.

- Asking for forgiveness when I have lied, covered up, and (often) "exaggerated the truth."
- Rationalizing the irrational choices I have made. Then blaming others for my actions.
- Justifying my actions because others do it.
- Making fun of others or myself as a "put down" and admitting this.
- Just being open to saying, "I love you" into a mirror and meaning it. Diving deeper into my feelings and emotions.
- Sitting with meditation and letting myself see the negative thoughts and beliefs I have believed in and how they have hurt others close to me. Then letting the tears flow down my face and over my chest. Then taking action to stand up for life inside *me* by being creative. Not letting my energy be wasted.
- Writing this book and gradually coming out as *me* with all my grey and black bits and colorful bits.
- Risking disapproval from family or friends.
- Admitting to my grown-up son and daughters that I am not just their dad, I am a vulnerable human being with many unexplored parts.
- Remembering those times when I have said something, but now wish I had kept my mouth shut.

Well I could go on. Maybe you could put this book down and write your vulnerabilities. You may be surprised.

Now I ask myself: *How does vulnerability feel in my mind body and soul?*

Here *goes*, Roger… now be truthful!" (A warning from my inner child to the inner parent that wants to cover up.)

- Feeling the way I'd feel being naked in front of thousands of laughing eyes. I want to dive for cover.
- Taking a huge leap of faith. Like coming here to Crete and spending money on me and writing this book.
- Just being seen through others' critical opinions of me.
- Feeling fearful and strong at the same time.

- Feeling relieved that I can take a deep breath!
- Feeling liberated to be me, despite what others think. Yet I do care not to go out of my way to hurt others involved.
- Being honest. For example, right now saying, "I want to leave a relationship of twenty-seven years!" To admit this to myself is the most difficult feeling in my mind, body, and spirit.
- Recognizing that vulnerability sometimes makes me feel that I want to die rather than face my truth.
- Worrying about the future when I wake up in the middle of the night and ponder on thoughts: Will I be ill? Who will look after me if I am single? Will there be enough money? Then my chatterbox goes ballistic! That is when I use positive affirmations to help me. They do not deny reality; rather, they truly help me create a much more safe and comforted place in *me*.
- Feeling my feelings are on show to everyone. And hearing old internalized records from childhood messages repeat themselves: "Be strong" when I feel so weak. I now know in my heart I am much more loveable to myself when I can feel my vulnerable feelings and let them through gently and with a kindness that surprises me.
- Acting totally inappropriately is one way to deal with vulnerable feelings; for example, if I want to say something difficult to a lover, I will choose to do it in public, like meet in a café, instead of privately because I am frightened of her anger.
- Acting in absurd ways to cover my feelings of weakness when I am triggered by my own memories of anger at *me*. If I see anger coming at me I want to protect myself. I will laugh instead of being centered. Or just be angry back and try to dominate and intimidate. This is changing as I write this. I am much more patient with this huge critical judge in me, as I love him gently out of me. I often laugh now with myself and let my inner critical parent rant privately and then just laugh at how funny I am. It's like seeing so clearly how I make my own reality beat me up, and then I change it! And I give thanks for new thoughts and beliefs. I can reprogram *me* beautifully!

- Pretending to listen, and actually stop listening, when I feel very vulnerable. This may be a common response, by men particularly, yet I am doing my best to overcome this. I do want to go to my cave! Yet that is now a beautiful retreat.

I believe that, if we are going to have a safer world in which to love and be loved, we need time to think well and share in a climate of appreciation.

One suggestion I have found so helpful for men is to share our thoughts and feelings with women. This is reflected in Nancy Kline's book, *Time to Think: Listening to Ignite the Human Mind*, and her later book, *More Time To Think*.

Simply put, Nancy gives human beings the vital luxury to practice appreciation after truly listening, without interruption, for a specified time to a loved one or work colleague. Nancy's wide-ranging work reveals our ability to create a climate that allows people to think in their own minds, which in turn creates a wisdom and honesty that we need to move our lives on in ways we have never dreamed of! Do read this book. People in my Heal Your Life groups have so benefited from Nancy's work. I often give business people the title of her books, and it's amazing how their meetings truly change toward deep wisdom and appreciation.

When we are listened to with incisive questions and we dissolve limiting assumptions about ourselves in a truly caring time frame, it's so nurturing to the inner genius in us all.

Contentment is a vital ingredient of wise love. Here's a story by Anthony De Mello, a Catholic priest who had a great way of making things simple out of what seemed complex philosophical ideas:

The Contented Fisherman

A rich man on holiday by the seaside came across a fisherman sitting beside his boat, smoking his pipe and drinking a cup of tea. "Why aren't you out fishing in your fine boat? It's a fine day and you could catch plenty of fish. You're just wasting valuable time sitting here idly like this," said the wealthy traveler.

"I've caught enough fish for today. Why do I need any more?" asked the fisherman.

"Well, more fish means more profit. You could sell your excess fish in the market, and after a while you would have enough money to buy yourself some bigger nets. That would allow you to catch even more fish. Then you could maybe buy a second boat and hire more men to work for you. Perhaps in ten years' time you might have a big house, nice clothes, and a lot of money in the bank," said the rich man, sticking out his chest.

"And what would I do then?"

"Then you'd really be able to take it easy and enjoy life!"

"What do you think I'm doing now?" asked the fisherman as he took another drink from his cup.

DIVE
10

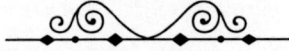

Lost and letting go

I sing a Donna De Lory song to myself—"Bathe in these Waters":

Lost! Criticized! Hard to reach! Hard to find! You will rise! I'll watch you fly! You will shine in time! Bathe in these waters and wash it away!

This is a song I have just put on after cycling up the mountain in the dusk of a beautiful warm, windy evening.

Fierce dive

My partner has just rung from the UK with her anger and hurt. While I listened, I caught my hand and foot on a wire fence, and blood flowed! I want to quote David Deida from his book *Finding God Through Sex: Awakening the One of Spirit Through the Two of Flesh*. The title made me slightly hesitant. I remember hiding it in my local café from searching eyes. The more I read his erotic and wise examples, the more daring and truthful I want to be. He puts my fear of a woman's anger and criticism into some perspective:

Some men can't handle their woman's anger. Other men shrink when their sexual, financial, or spiritual capacities are criticized. Most men crumble when their woman doesn't

acknowledge their success in the project that is so dear to them.
Other men are terrified of their woman's emotional chaos. You
know what your man most fears and you know how to give it
to him.

So I need to learn how to handle this energy from my primary
partner. I ask myself, "Can I absorb her anger or criticism, and determine
what is true and useful—and freely make the changes?" Otherwise, as
David puts it:

But if he is not ready to change, then your heavy, angry, or
shut down energy becomes a pure burden in his life. Whereas
the fundamental feminine bad mood is the feeling of being
unloved, the fundamental masculine bad mood is the feeling
of being burdened.

This resonates with me. Yet David gives hope to us men in terms of
learning "deep being"!

Your man can learn to discover the freedom and openness of
deep being. Then he won't blame you for burdening him, nor
will your attempts at "hurting him back" have much effect on
him. He'll embrace you in real love, and if you continue to bitch
for too long he will lovingly let you go and move on.

I suppose I know my partner wants to punish me, and she has every
right in some ways, yet I know too that a deeper part of her heart is
filled with compassion. She knows she is love, loving, and loveable—so
too am I. We know this so intimately. I know I am going through my
lessons, and she hers. Whether we come back to each other depends on
whether we collapse into victimhood. Well, I choose to be full of radiant
love and full of energy. And I know my partner can choose that. She
said, "I have been dying over the past five years." I would rather leave
and see her thrive in the fullness of her love of life, than be a constant
burden to her and see her die spiritually, sexually, and emotionally. I do

want us to be true friends and be together at times with all the family. (Back in the UK. Just listened to BBC Radio 4 on Woman's Hour about how so many couples, gay or straight, have become true friends after separation.)

From this intention and disposition I can bless my partner and remember the beautiful wild passion we shared. I can slow down and reclaim my heart. The "deep being" in me can go beyond hurt and pain and dissolve the past with tears of happiness and forgiveness. I can lose the "charge" on my memories of hurt. This is so freeing for moving on.

Facing *me*

Eileen Caddy, founding member of Findhorn community said, *"learn your lessons quickly and move on!"*

I now feel lost, yet somehow found, and in need of facing the man in the mirror of life. Yet, from what I have learned from all the books and therapy, I don't need to be a victim. I can face life with an open, forgiving heart and be human and face the opinions of others without blame or feeling so wrong. I could seek a psychiatrist who would give me tablets and a simplistic label.

When I give talks to this profession I ask, If you had a "break open" to your truth—what you call a "breakdown"—would you seek your own counsel for treatment? Never has any psychiatrist put up his or her hand and said yes! What does this say about our drug companies and their "mind control" over the psychiatric profession?

I am an empowered, deeply spiritual man who needs to heal his secret life. I can honestly reply (without ego) to the question I ask the psychiatrists, "I would welcome the chance to go to an open-minded counselor (like myself) who would truly listen to my darkest secrets, be there as an empowering mirror, and give me real time to heal from the inside to out."

To change, we *men* need to feel safe as individuals! Often women tell me, "I wish 'my man' could come and talk with you, Roger. He is so cut off from everyone—including me." And they often add (as if I could wave a magic wand), "If only he could talk emotionally with feelings, I could love him more!" I can hear one of my old Buddhist teacher's reply, *"If you want him to change, become like the person you would like to fall in love with! Stop changing him! Just be in love with* you *and create what you want in him, in you; you become those qualities! Then see how loving he becomes! If there is no change, then you have a choice!"*

This can sound politically incorrect, yet if we force men (and women) to change, we so often dig our heels in, and resistance follows.

Growing climates that create intimacy with love

I ask myself: *What helps me change positively and authentically as a person—not just as a man?*

I feel comfortable changing when I will be listened to without interruption, then appreciated. If I hear women "bashing and blaming" men as if we are some demonic herd of animals, I feel so powerless. It's like ripping my heart out, and I want to run like the male child I talked of earlier. I know we men have done so much that has been—and still is—so inhuman, yet we are not to be grouped together like some evil creation. Please experience us as individuals. We can change for the better, if we are allowed to be truly heard and then responded to with an open heart.

When I am listened to with patience, I am able to feel deeper layers of past conditioning. This in turn helps me catch and match the subtle and deeply moving vibrations of a feeling and emotional woman in her thoughts and feelings.

When we humans give ourselves "time to think" with the intention to honor ourselves and each other, then even potential conflict can be dissolved by careful, empathic listening.

What helps me to be transparent in relationships is pinpointing from my history, where the original pain of rejection, criticism and fear built my emotional armor. This amour helped me survive, but got in the way to be truly alive to what is going on now. This can sound like an excuse, yet to be listened to so silently and empathically brings wisdom and truth to awareness.

If I am listened to with a high degree of impatience and judgment, it reinforces old self-protection patterns of behavior. An example is a curt statement, such as: "Oh, not that old excuse again!"

When either a man or a woman judges with impatience, I believe we do go to our respective caves—or to the fridge to stuff the feelings down!

Give me time to find the emotional language that I am grasping for, because that will help me to go deeper to my reality inside. When a person I want to connect to is listening with judgment and impatience with constant interruptions and explains my emotional reality back to me, I will shut off and let them describe my reality for me. The only problem here is, I will build resentment and dig a hole between us. Give real time to listen both ways. I love feeling "disarming empathy" by just listening from a deep place. It opens new doors to understanding myself.

I realize, as a man, that I think of consciousness and spirituality through words, books, and discussions, as something associated with my head. This can be a mistake. I see how often I mismatch a women's understanding of consciousness, which is much more about light, energy, and feeling, rather than heady rationalizing. I realize this is a generalization, yet to listen without interruption and vice versa, with genuine appreciation at the end, is like making love so deeply to yourself and your partner without any genital penetration.

I have learned to adore a woman for her beauty and being the main attraction in my life. And if I am honest, I love a woman to love my genitals and treat me as a god! This is difficult to write; yet I love to honor the goddess of a woman's genitals and her whole being. Now, that might get your thoughts going! Yet what really helps me to get close to a woman is surrendering to *her ability to allow deep affirming emotions to flow in love-making.*

You may say that's my ego speaking and very macho, yet I believe if we feel good about the beauty of our bodies and including our wonderful genitals, (whatever size) our self-worth hums with delight! For my part I am learning to surrender to love through my whole body and breath—not just with my genitals. I am learning to feel that my whole sexuality is so close to the divine love in every part of life—seen and unseen.

What helps me feel safe and not frightened, is creating real time to "becoming a person", not just being seen and experienced as a "problem"! If we men are just seen by others and experienced by ourselves as problems, and continually blamed, I feel sad for the future of our world. Let us learn to be *warriors* of love—not war! In my experience, when men and women feel truly safe to share without critical analysis and interruptions then intimacy truly builds inside and out.

As a man, I want to be part of a movement that can build person-centered listening climates that help men change with love and creative wisdom. So we become *warrior* listeners and lovers, to anyone with mutual respect, between the sexes, then real positive, long-lasting, change will happen. I see women have built beautiful ways of connecting to other women. Now men can be truly powerful as we learn a whole new emotional language of intimacy. We may not replicate the strength of women's circles, yet men can learn from other men beautifully, when father-son issues are shared and healed by our combined male empathic and softer strength. I have witnessed men truly move, and dissolve rocks of hurt and pain, when they talk about father issues with other men who listen without any interruption. And then show genuine appreciation.

I am reminded of a little spiritual story:

Using All Your Strength

A young boy and his father were walking together when they came across a large stone in the middle of the road. "That's dangerous," said the father. "It needs to be moved."

"Do you think I could move it if I used all my strength?" asked the boy.

"If you use all your strength, I'm sure you'll be able to move it," replied the father.

The young lad placed his two hands on the rock and began to push. The rock didn't move. Then, instead of pushing, he pulled. No success. He found a stick and tried to use it as a lever, *but that was ineffective.* "You were wrong," said the boy to his father. "I can't move it."

"But you didn't use all your strength."

"Yes I did. I tried as hard as I could."

"But there was one thing you didn't do."

"What's that?"

"You didn't ask me for help!" said the father with a smile.

(From David J. Wolpe's book, *Teaching Your Children About God: A Modern Jewish Approach.*)

I know I need wise women to help *me* be *me*. And I suspect that could smack of codependency; yet, I want to be a friend, not an enemy. I believe that most males want this! We learned so early to isolate ourselves. Come out, men, and risk being vulnerable and so loveable!

I love the song "Where Is the Love?" by the Black Eyed Peas. It is a song that asks so many questions about the truth that is kept from us—or that we deny, even when we know the truth. So I ask, where is your love? We need some guidance from above. So now I ask the stars and dark night, Bring me love! So many shooting stars tonight. Good night to you all.

A short story before bed:

Heaven and Hell

Once, a samurai swordsman went to visit a holy man called Hakuin. "Sir, please tell me, are heaven and hell real, or are they just a figment of our imagination?" he asked.

Hakuin was silent for a few minutes, and then he said, "Who are you?"

"I am a samurai warrior, a member of the king's personal guard. I have been trained in the art of warfare, and I am one of the most accomplished swordsmen in the whole country," replied the samurai proudly.

"I don't believe it," said Hakuin with a smile. "You don't look strong enough to hurt a fly! You look more like a beggar than a soldier."

At this insult, the warrior's face grew red, and he instinctively went for his sword.

"Oh, you have a sword do you? I'll bet it's not sharp enough to cut off my little finger!" said Hakuin, shaking his head in disdain.

The samurai couldn't contain his anger any longer, and he drew his sword, ready to strike off Hakuin's head. Without flinching, Hakuin looked first at the sword poised for action, and then fixing his gaze firmly on the soldier's eyes, he said, "That is hell."

The soldier, realizing what Hakuin was trying to teach him, put his sword back in its sheath.

"And that," said Hakuin, "is heaven."

DIVE

11

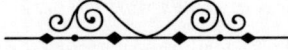

Dream a dream that is love, not fear

My Louise Hay affirmation card today is: *"It is safe for me to look within. Each time I look deeper into myself, I will find incredibly beautiful treasures within me."*

Good morning wherever you are. I have awakened with a lion roaring inside my dream state. It was Konstantina's beautiful dog barking me awake on this sun-soaked morning in Crete. My first thoughts were, *I am alive and open to divine inspiration!* After a fruit breakfast, I play the song "Boogie Street" by Leonard Cohen.

I'm on my way out to dance and sing on the villa's tiled plateau. Then I'll do yoga and listen with meditation to screeching cicadas. There is such a healing in "the power of beauty" that surrounds me.

Last night, sitting under the vast starry night, I gently asked, "What am I here for? What do you want me to be? Who am I?"

My eyes started to cry with beautiful memories of this life. I shouted to every star: "Are we wonderful wounded people? Have we forgotten that we are such miracles of light and love? Please come and be in me in my sleep and let me find that vast infinite wisdom that made all your universes! Help me write with such integrity!"

As Don Miguel Ruiz succinctly puts it in his book, *The Mastery of Love*:

> *The happiest moments in our life are when we are playing just like children, when we are singing and dancing, when we are exploring and creating just for fun. It is wonderful when we*

behave like a child because this is the normal human mind potential.

When we play like children, the parasite of fear cannot take root, the dream of love is still alive, and our negatively conditioned adult, parents and teachers, whose examples are highly contagious, have not dulled us into submission. I love watching my children and my son-in-law John. They are all now "grown up" and are still so inquisitive and creative as they play often with laughter. I feel so heartened by the young people I meet as a DJ; the eternal child in me meets their dancing spirit!

Listening to the song: "I'm Yours" by Jason Mraz. Nobody can own or control us, yet we can feel connected by such loving thoughts and actions to the vast number of souls on this earth. I now know that what I choose to think connects me to others somewhere on this planet.

I love to "radiate love" wherever I go during each day. This has moved me from the domesticated mistrusting adult to connecting with people with compassion. Do you realize your love is limitless as you build more unconditional love in your heart? I suggest the more you love *you*, the easier it will be to feel good and happy, even when tough experiences appear: *"People's opinions are not important. They are not important because we just want to play and we live in the present."*—Don Miguel Ruiz

Imagine if this thought created your life, and your "inner genius" child could feel that love is in the air with every breath that you breathe, every moment of your life.

"Love Is in the Air." Imagine us dancing to this song. What would every cell in our bodies celebrate with this thought and belief, instead of the idea that we are not good enough? I know it may be romantic to suggest such a thought as love is in the air!

Imagine taking "love is in the air!" as your mantra. Our breath is so precious, so why not dream the whisper of love being in every breath. How beautifully promiscuous air is, once it is in my lungs, then in yours. We are so connected by the soles of our feet on planet Earth and by our breath.

I am often criticized for being too simplistic, yet through forty-three years of counseling, I have found that when human beings rebirth their genius child (by learning to build a truly nurturing inner parent!) they learn to play and find a peace; they heal so fast and have fun. As Eileen Caddy suggests, *"Seek always for the answers within. Be not influenced by those around you, by their thoughts or words."*

Dance for life

When I dance to beautiful music it feels like dancing with my maker."
I am privileged to facilitate, on Sunday afternoons, Dance for Life sessions, based on *fluid and free movement where feelings and emotions come to the surface without judgment.* The dance takes us through beautiful music. This opens up people's need for freedom of movement on all levels, especially emotion and spirit wisdom. The music and free

movement explores synergy and creativity and reduces resistance, so our heart expands. The heart cannot resist *you* loving *you* in the dance. All parts of you respond, especially when you dance to bone-and-blood joyous music. The music of love inside of us bypasses the mind and delves deeply to being in the *now* with your *body*. Dance in any way where you imagine *there is no right or wrong*.

The beat of drums has the same resonance the divine uses to knock on the walls of your heart. When this happens you go into deeper levels of flow. And when you move, you move as if a free spirit feeds your soul. Inspiration comes into thought, emotion, and feeling. The force is with you and in you! So many people tell me they can't dance. I just bypass this negative affirmation and hold their hands and gently take them onto the floor. It's amazing that the impulse to run transforms into a desire to move and dance.

The difficult edges of embarrassment disappear, and a whole well of tears surfaces in the dance. It's like making love with yourself and others with your clothes on. The flirt, the wild goddess or god, comes into the dance. Your blood boils, your breath goes deeper, there is no guilt … just a deeper truth to find and explore.

I get such inspiration from the energy on the floor as dancers start to touch and roll on the floor, like a new child being born. And then I play the next track that falls into my mind as I open out my arms wide. I am a dancing DJ! I love it, and I do it with as much love as the divine wants to pass through me.

Dance—even if you are in a wheel chair. When I watched my friend Chris dance in his wheel chair at my sixty-fifth birthday, I cried with delight. He had just come out of a spinal injury unit for the first time. For a moment I saw the whole divine presence light up the divine gestalt around him as he struggled to remember his love of ecstatic dance. I love your courage, Chris.

Attracting flow into your heart

When I'm in the flow of life, I find that people who are inspired cross my path. An example: I have just watched a YouTube video of the documentary *Fat Sick & Nearly Dead*. It made me cry! One man, Joe, decided to change his eating habits and took to vegetable juicing. He travelled through the United States meeting people like him— so overweight. He then met a lorry driver who eventually asked Joe for help.

The true story shows how, when we wake up to the parasite of fear killing us, we can bring back our dream of loving life and touching others for good in the process. I see that overeating the wrong foods to feed our beautiful bodies is such a painful way of hiding ourselves from a deep feeling that we are not good enough.

Have you ever listened to Bobby Womac's song, "Love Is Gonna Lift You Up"? It makes me want to dance naked to the breeze and to the wild hot sun. Then, as if magic stirs my heart, the next track is "Listen to the Breeze" by Chiwoniso. Synchronicity comes to this magical breeze coming through the trees and wild, sunburned mountains. I quote:

> *I know this old man. He lives in a house on the hill. Each day I pass him sitting there rocking on his chair. I lift my hand in greeting, he smiles in return. Then one day he says: "Come here child, I have words to tell. I will share secrets you have never heard before. There is magic in the air. All you do is listen to the breeze!*

So I listen to the breeze and let go of burdens that keep my heart from opening to the truth of who I am.

I hope you can dance even in your wheel chair or if you're lying in an institution of despair, like prison, or if you're in a job you need to leave. Just open yourself to new miracles of life. You may be in a relationship that fills you with stuck energy. Just invite your mind to open by opening your arms wide and saying, "I am open and receptive to all good!" And then give thanks for what you cannot see yet. My love and support to you. You can change your life as you choose to watch what you are thinking, and saying, then with increased awareness choose love in every feeling thought!

DIVE
12

Good morning! My Louise Hay card this morning: *"I rejoice in my employment—there are people looking for exactly what I have to offer, and we are being brought together on the checkerboard of life."*

I have awakened to the sun coming up over the olive trees and Cat Stevens singing "Morning has Broken." I feel fresh and beautiful and ready to write with divine inspiration.

I am reminded of the Native American story and it goes like this:

Feeding the Wolf

"Why is it that sometimes I feel that I want to do helpful things, but at other times I just want my own way?" a little Cherokee boy asked his grandfather one day.

"It's because there is a battle between two wolves. One wolf is kind and gentle, full of peace, generosity, compassion, and trust. The other is wicked, full of anger, hatred, greed, selfishness, pride, and arrogance."

The young boy thought for a moment, and then he asked, "Which one will win the battle inside me?"

"The one you feed," replied his grandfather.

Insight: Sometimes in my life I have fed the so-called wicked wolf, even while knowing there is a kind wolf inside me. This creates such a fight in me, my chatterbox, or inner conversation, goes wild. When I give talks to groups or run Heal Your Life sessions, I know I act in spirit and with inspired connections to the god inside, and this brings the kind, loving wolf into being.

God is love, and love is God

As I write, tears flow. I am listening to Maneesh de Moor playing a piano version of "Let it Be." The album is *Eckhart Tolle's Music to Quiet the Mind*. I realize that a whole section of my life is coming to an end, and I need to "let it be" and let go with love.

I am reminded of Deepak Chopra's line in his fabulous book *The Path to Love*: "*Every time you are tempted to react in the same old way, ask yourself if you want to be a prisoner of the past or a pioneer of the future. The past is closed and limited; the future is open and free.*"

As I sit here, high in the mountains, and look with my inner eye at rugged beauty and hear the muffled ringing of the goats' bells, I feel as if my spirit blends into the valleys and flows with passionate love. The rising sun and freshening wind take me into God's grace. I want to carry you with me. It feels so natural here to be spiritual and to feel love is only natural. Being in the "power of now" I feel the heart of God so close to mine. It feels as if this is the first time I have seen your face!

You may think I am on some drug. I am just finding my kind, loving wolf that loves to be fed!

As psychologist and author Robert Holden wrote:

> *Forgiveness undoes the blocks to love's awareness. It shows you that a universe of love doesn't ever stop, even when all you can see is pain. Love always loves you, even when you can't or won't love yourself.*

DIVE

13

Transformation through listening

I love saying, "Today I will meet the right people and radiate love wherever I go."

On the coach coming over the mountains, I listened to a young woman named Julie. She told me her story. She was a frustrated German business student, and had come to Crete years ago as a child. Julie gradually trusted me and went deep into her past and recounted her relationships and her dreams of doing something worthwhile. Her spirit was heavy, and her words tumbled out like accusations at herself and life. I asked her, "What are your dreams?" She replied, "Wow, very few people ask that question—especially at college!"

Yet, as she sat back, feeling slightly coach sick, she suddenly remembered a dream of being close to the land and growing vegetables and living in a community. I suggested a lovely documentary, *One Man, One Cow, One Planet*. At the end of the coach journey, she took my card, and I also suggested she read Louise Hay's *You Can Heal Your Life*. Then she went on her way with her two German friends. I am not writing about this to blow my own trumpet; it is simply an example of putting love into action. I remember Ole Larson, a teacher at the Institute for Self-Actualization (ISA). He asked me, "Do people leave you feeling better for having met you, or worse?"

Meetings are so wonderful when I embrace the intention just to listen and appreciate. We can all remember, I am sure, special people who have listened to us and given us help just at the right time and in the perfect space sequence. I am blessed with so many people who have loved being with me on my journey. Just listen to the song "Lean on Me" by Bill Withers: *"We all need somebody to lean on!"* My fingers are tapping to the music. I love how to love life and to be in that stream or flow. And the song ends, *"Just call me if you need a friend!"*

Then I listen to Sweet Honey in the Rock singing "I Like It That Way" And the verse goes on:

> *Is everybody ready? Then we are going to sing a song about how much we like ourselves, because it's so good to be the wonderful, glorious intelligent, creative person you are each and every day! Let me hear those honey horns.*

The healing power of soul music

Music crosses so many barriers in such a disarming way. I love how World of Music, Arts and Dance (WOMAD) music festivals and many festivals like the Gaia festivals are surging through all countries. I believe so many souls travel to such festivals to meet a need to love, dance, and learn new skills.

I have encouraged my small family, with my wife supporting me, to attend such camps and festivals. The people you meet are doing their best to educate children outside rigid school systems and have many skills that convert life into an adventure. When I went to New Zealand at age twenty-nine and lived in a Quaker community, I realized how many practical skills I had missed learning as a child of the '50s and '60s. We were so fixed on getting a good education rather than being truly whole human beings.

I do encourage parents to take children to places that involve a new type of awareness and consciousness. Then we can truly help future generations to heal our planet.

This reminds me of another wolf story. This one's about freedom:

The Wolf and the Dog

One day, a dog met a wolf in the forest. The dog said to the wolf, "Mr. Wolf, why are you so thin? Haven't you eaten recently? You must learn to look after yourself better."

"I eat when I can," said the wolf, "but it's not always easy to get food. I'm getting older, and I'm not as quick as I used to be. The animals I eat seem to be able to get away from me these days."

"You should come and live with me," said the dog. "I live in a big house; it's warm and cozy; my master feeds me three times every day; and I can sit and doze in front of the fire any time I like. Sometimes he lets me out for a few minutes so I can run around the forest. There he is, over there waiting for me to go back to him. Come with me. He'll look after you."

"I think I will," replied the wolf. "Why should I be out here in the cold, grabbing what food I can, when I can be fed for free? Lead the way."

As the dog went on ahead, the wolf noticed that the dog had a little circle round his neck where the fur had worn away.

"What's wrong with your neck?" he asked.

"Oh it's nothing. It's just where my master fastens a chain around me each night to keep me in my place while he is asleep," said the dog, a little ashamed.

"Sorry," said the wolf. "I won't be coming with you. I'd rather be half starved and free than well fed and a slave. Goodbye." And the wolf vanished into the forest.

I ask you and myself, "Do I want to be free or comfortable?" Many of my clients over the years have told me they live in homes, yet they are in relationships that are abusive or emotionally poisoned, and they believe that they must always live with a chain around their minds, bodies, and spirits.

I believe we have to become more conscious; otherwise, we stay in hurt and pain.

DIVE

14

In his book, *Kinship with All Life*, J. Allen Boone wrote, *"If you would learn the secret of right relations, look only for the divine in people and things, and leave all the rest to God."*

Open Marriage: A New Life Style for Couples by Nena O'Neill and George O'Neill is a wonderfully insightful book, written in 1972, because it provides a refreshing, well-researched perspective on intimate relationships that may or may not involve sex outside marriage. Looking back (and I am sure you have often thought this), I wish I had read this book years ago. It may have saved my marriage.

The O'Neills write about "fidelity redefined." Let me quote at some length:

> *Sexual fidelity is the false god of closed marriage, a god to whom partners submit (or whom they defy) for all the wrong reasons and often at the cost of the very relationship which that god is supposed to protect. Sex in the closed marriage is envisioned in terms of fidelity, thus becoming the be-all and end-all of love, instead of being seen in its proper perspective as only one facet of the much larger reality of love. Fidelity in the closed marriage is the measure of limited love, diminished growth and conditional trust. This fixation in the end defeats its own purpose, encouraging deception, sowing seeds of mistrust and limiting growth of both partners and so of the love between them.*

Then they say clearly:

> *Fidelity, in its root meaning, denotes allegiance and fealty to a duty or obligation. But love and sex should never be seen in terms of duty or obligation, as they are in closed marriage. They should be seen as experiences to be shared and enjoyed together, as they are in open marriage, as commitment to your own growth, equal commitment to your partner's growth, and a sharing of the self-discovery accomplished through such growth. It is* loyalty and faithfulness to growth, *[my emphasis]* to integrity of self and respect for the other, not to a sexual and psychological bondage to each other.

I know that each partner needs to be secure in his or her own identity, and each must trust in the other in order that new possibilities for additional relationships can exist.

Maybe we are ready when we are ready. Not everyone is suited to an open marriage, and the O'Neills never force this view of marriage. I believe open marriage has ushered in a new age, if people truly understand it, where illicit affairs and prudish "arrangements" are no longer the only choices for those desiring freedom with honesty and responsibility. So I do suggest to you, read this book carefully. Remember it's not about sex; it's about two people growing with honesty and integrity.

Compersion or jealousy?

A few years ago, I attended a polyamory workshop where I heard the word *compersion*. It was created by the Kerista Community to describe an emotion that is opposite to jealousy. Let me quote Dr. Deborah Anapol's *Polyamory in the 21st Century: Love and Intimacy with Multiple Partners*: "*Compersion means to feel joy and delight when one's beloved loves or is being loved by another.*" She goes on to say:

> *However, since most of us have been raised with an expectation of jealousy, compersion is an alien concept. Learning theory tells*

> *us that it's always easier to replace one habit with another than to just eliminate the first one.*

I know for me it was a revelation that I could learn gradually to dissolve jealousy. I know that I learned extreme jealousy from two jealous parents. So for me, freeing myself from jealousy is a big jump, yet it is vital, I believe, to becoming more open to growth and unconditional love.

So once we start reading or listening to good knowledge and develop awareness coupled with growing skills and a willpower that gives us enthusiasm (finding the god within), then I see people taking back their miraculous healing power and choosing an intention that is uniquely creative and connects to running free with genuine love in the forest of life! As an aside, I have often wondered if one of my past lives was a North American Indian, running wild and free.

Insight: If we bury ourselves in ignorance and still have secret affairs, the lies will carry on. I believe if we adults could only learn compersion (an empathetic state of happiness and joy experienced when another individual experiences happiness and joy) and reduce jealousy, then children would learn it so much more easily. We cannot stop new awareness if we are committed to growth. It is possible to feel joy and expansion rather than fear and contraction in response to a loved one sharing his or her love with others. However, it's not always easy! Could we use our jealousy as a pathway to learning unconditional love?

I fully realize we would have to consider how we talk about and demonstrate this type of love and living to children.

Just turned to the book *Heart Thoughts*

Louise Hay wrote, *"Each of us is doing the very best we can at this very moment. If we knew better, if we had more understanding and awareness, we would do it differently."*

Turning our flaws into strengths!

I feel my life is likened to the story of the cracked pot, a Hindu tale. I remember telling this story at one of my book launches, because I think it describes many souls on their journey, including me!

The Cracked Pot

Many years ago in India, a certain servant made a daily visit to a well to bring water for his master's household. He brought the water in two large pots hung on either end of a pole he carried across his shoulders.

One of the pots was flawless and never spilled a drop of water, but the other one had a small crack in the bottom and so, at the end of the servant's two-mile walk from the well, it was only half full.

The perfect pot was very proud of its ability to deliver a full quota of water, but the pot with the crack was ashamed of its imperfections, and one day it spoke to the water carrier. "I want to apologize for being so useless," it said. "Because of me, you don't get the full value of your work. I'm letting you down."

The water carrier felt sorry for the leaking pot, and he replied with a smile, "As we go back to the master's house, I want you to look at the beautiful flowers along the path."

The cracked pot did as he was asked. The servant was right; there were beautiful flowers along the path, and the old pot was cheered a little by the sight, but the flowers didn't make him happy or feel any better about himself. In fact, in some ways, they made him feel worse; after all, they were colorful and fragrant, whereas he was old and leaky.

When they got back to the house, the pot still felt sad because he was only half full, and it apologized once again for its imperfections. "Did you look at the beautiful flowers on the path as I asked you to?" asked the servant.

"Yes I did. They are lovely, but they made me even more aware of my flaw," said the cracked pot sadly.

"Did you notice that they were only on one side of the path—the side I carry you on? I've known about your flaw for a long time, and I took advantage of it. I planted some flower seeds on your side of the path, and now each day as I come back from the well, your leak waters the flowers. Each day I pick some of the flowers that have grown so well because of you, and use them to decorate our master's dinner table. Without you being just as you are, we wouldn't have such beauty in the house."

This story is an antidote to the cult of perfection. Most of my clients have learned to see their flaws as strengths. I like that, because those are the people who become so much more loveable.

DIVE

15

~~~

"One Day Like This" is a song by Elbow. I often play it at the end of a Dance for Life session, when I see people "throw those curtains wide" from mind, body, and soul. I experience what Greg Bradon calls the "divine matrix." I see the force of love and forgiveness go in every direction at the same time. I can feel such an intimate connection among all the dancers as we "sweat our prayers" (Gabrielle Roth: Sweat Your Prayers) and cry out for healing our relationships, especially the one with ourselves.

Jealousy is so often about fear of being abandoned

I have married twice, and I have had many other relationships. So often I have said, "Never again!" The hurt was too much. I hated feeling so disappointed, devastated, and broken hearted.

It's taken me ages to reach some lighter feelings around relationships. My present partner says, I am so intense. Well, as we part, I am living in this mountain retreat doing my best to enlighten myself and work out what's going on. Now I am gradually learning that I need to clear old beliefs and the poison of a parasite that tells me I am not good at relationships! So my affirmation is: "I will not abandon myself; I am here for *me*."

I would love to believe what Sandra Ray says: *"I know that there is a new way to handle relationships, a way that always brings me peace and joy and enlightenment no matter what happens."*

This is my intention. I know things out there are always mirrors of what's going on in here.

I am letting go of what others may think and what my past has molded me into. I want a self that is permanent and can live in the *now* and drink in life without always crumpling into devastation. I want to handle jealousy and grow old with grace.

Sondra Ray quotes Kyle Os' definition of loving relationships *When one partner does not interfere with the other's love for him/herself."*

Handling my jealousy

I know you may have experienced gut-wrenching feelings when you knew your partner was with someone else. When it happens to me, I feel that my entire world goes into chaos, and I can't think clearly. Everything—including my car—goes wrong!

I have changed from a strictly monogamous relationship to an open relationship, yet I have never really faced up to my feelings as a man sharing my partner with other lovers. Now is the time to be honest.

You can read many books and still feel confused about how to handle relationships, and especially jealousy. You have your unique way. All I know from years of counseling is that most people have secret affairs and are never truthful to their main partners. But who am I—or you—to judge?

We all need to be honest when we change from monogamous to open relationships, and maybe back again, and find ways to express feelings safely when jealousy erupts. Spiritual leader Sondra Ray asks this question to a person experiencing jealousy: *"Why did you set up a jealousy situation in the first place?"* In other words, what's the payoff?

Then she asks a whole list of questions. These are some on her list to ask yourself, and they are pertinent to me as well:

1. Did I attract this situation to prove I wasn't good enough?
2. Was my relationship getting too good and too close so I had to destroy it?
3. Am I addicted to pain, and do I love it?
4. Am I hooked on drama rather than peace?

5. Was I getting more love than I deserved, so that I had to get rid of it?
6. Am I using this mess so I can get rid of my partner?
7. Do I love to punish myself with this because I have guilt about something?

Sandra is very clear that each of us must take responsibility for our jealousy, because somewhere we actually take part in setting it up!

She is also clear that we need to set up win-win circumstances that suit both partners in a loving relationship, whether it is open or monogamous. "There are no "shoulds" or "supposed tos.""

Getting older as a man with good health and positive consciousness

For me, being alone for a few weeks while I write this book is part of a healthy process of working with myself, and changing my beliefs and consciousness. I need to take responsibility in my life with self-love and self-esteem. When I experience positive self-worth, I can truly be me. I want to get old with dignity—not be a "grumpy old man"! I want to look at aging differently. I quote Wayne Dyer: *"Change the way you look at things and the things you look at will change."*

I have arrived at the idea of leading Heal Your Life workshops in as many places as possible, and working specifically with men. However, not to the exclusion of women. I want to live and think outside the box. I do not want to be a burden on my family. I want to keep learning. I want to meditate on love. I want to teach others. I want to keep my body in good shape. I have learned yoga, and it helps me prepare well for each day.

Sometimes I think I need many relationships; at other times I want to be alone. I will always place myself in positions where I can get the lessons I need to learn. Stillness is so important to me at this moment in time. I will be honest; different relationships bring out unknown parts of me. Some are truly amazing aspects of myself, while other mirrors are deeply challenging. The worst part for me is running from one relationship to another. This creates chaos and hurt.

I would love to travel and visit worldwide Heal Your Life communities and share living spaces around the world. In those places we could take our unique skills and assist each other in growth! (A bit like "woofing"—helping out, under the auspices of Worldwide Opportunities on Organic Farms, on ecological permaculture sites around the world.)

I realize I have lessons to learn about my spiritual journey and lessons to TEACH others who are willing to learn.

DIVE

16

Sexuality with spirituality

In her book, *Spiritual Sex (Undercover Sex Tips)*, Michelle Pauli wrote, *"In orgasm we glimpse eternity —a sense of something greater than ourselves and earthly pleasures—and experience a timelessness and oneness with the universe."*

Let me say it straight: I am no expert on sex and spirituality. Yet these feel so important to most people in this life, especially those wonderful hurt people I have listened too as a therapist in my little garden hut.

Please hear this: I am a polyamorist, but that doesn't mean that I go around having free sex with everybody I want. I am saying our present rules around marriage and relationships can make us lie and cheat on our primary relationships. If we remove sexual guilt by teaching people to love themselves from a place of authenticity, where there are fewer lies and cover-ups, we will treat others and ourselves with more respect.

One book that opens beautiful aspects of love, sex, and spirituality is *The Path To Love* by Deepak Chopra.

Suggestion: Just allow yourself to read this book and where it falls open, will be a possible lesson to learn.

I feel genuinely privileged to hear the heartache of men and women who are struggling to love their bodies as they work toward enjoying their sexuality. As a man, in the past when I felt unsafe, I have needed to prove myself in sex.

When I feel I cannot meet a woman's needs sexually and emotionally, I know I need to stop sex and reflect on how my past emotional patterns are surfacing during the act of intimacy.

It is strange we so rarely talk to anyone about one of the most pleasurable and joyous acts, which is also, I believe, deeply spiritual. We can find the divine in wonderful spiritual and sexual union.

The joy of sexual union

Let me dive deeper. I am a very physical person who loves and sometimes craves touch. I love giving and receiving touch. My body becomes slightly animalistic in a sensitive way. To penetrate a woman is such a beautiful act if I honor her and myself, and she honors herself and me. It is not just our genitals. It is about a truly deep act of energies coming together and creating a wave of complete bliss. I have often been with women whom I cannot penetrate physically or emotionally, and we have just been naked together as friends.

When I feel a deep conversation and sharing on all levels, and I inhale the smell of skin, and I look at eyes that look deep into my soul, then I give myself to the beauty of sex. As a male with usually a lot of energy for life and making love, I feel a deep spiritual connection. The pleasure and joy of deep, exploring kisses is like rebirth and completion. It feels like breathing in life for the first time. All the sexual and physical positions are wonderful, yet to be so close and be penetrated and penetrating is such a joy for me. It is always a new experience. Sex is never the same, no matter how often I have made love with the same woman.

When we love ourselves and we come from truly good intentions, I believe we attract alike. Our bodies become like magnets. When I met my present partner, all we wanted to do was make love. We just made a "beeline" for each other. I felt like wine after years of storage being drunk at its best time. When I meet a woman who gives off such inner beauty and allows laughter and tears to mix in her pleasure, the sexual act is like a massive transition into a new world that explodes my whole body. When I find ecstasy in making love, my mind and body become *one* with my soul.

Richard Gentle (spiritual writer). His name reflects a wise searching soul who loves to serve by writing self-help books with a deep spiritual wisdom) wrote this on the differences in intimacy between men and women – though he admits this particular thought is a generalization:

> *"In my own observation, it appears in many cases, women approach intimacy through "emotional feeling" before becoming physical and men approach sex through "physical feeling" before becoming emotional."*

Freddy the dolphin—another teacher

I went swimming with Freddy the Dolphin in Northumberland. Let me tell you, going one morning every week to swim in the sea with a dolphin totally changed my sex and spiritual life. I went with my family to Northumberland to swim with Freddy.

Let me explain. I was a member of International Dolphin Watch. Horace Dobbs, who ran the watch in my area, had been asked by a light keeper to take a fisherman's hook out of Freddy's fin. After this was accomplished, Freddy became attuned to the sound of the boat's engine, and each time the light keeper's boat went out into the ocean, Freddy associated the sound with healing love! How advanced is that in consciousness? He would swim alongside the boat, wanting someone to play with him and love him. So there I was ready to dive in wearing my wetsuit, and there was Freddy waiting. I dived in feeling the whole universe was about to collapse around me. What I found was instant connection with trust and love at our first connection. He looked through me and saw my beauty. In him, I saw a magnificent energy for love and gentleness. We swam, and then he rolled over and showed me his beautiful penis. He had no shame or guilt; he just wanted to experience fun and the joy of playing in the now.

What trust he gave me. At that point, I put my arms around him and he took me out to sea away from the boat. And we played—or, really, he showed off. He dived down deep and came a few feet from me and threw himself over me. His streaming and glistening body was converted into complete joy, which gave me ecstasy. The joy of his sexual energy gave me a direct experience of what it is to be at *one* with another wise and totally loving mind, body, and soul.

Freddy was a deeply spiritual and wise being. I loved him, and he loved me. I know as I write this that I carry his love within me. He gave me a gift of bliss when I took the risk to dive deep into the unknown. I felt totally safe with his energy, which is what women and men have told me when they have truly good sex—long or short sex. It's like being on the edge of orgasms. Freddy gave to me a gift; my experience with him taught me to face fears and convert the risk of diving into those fears and finding spiritual love.

I hope when I make and receive love, I pass on this quality of energy to the women I love. Anyway, if I leave this training ground today, I hope I pass this on to you.

Freddy would not let me go until I stroked his nose with my foot. In my counseling hut I have a huge picture of Freddy and I swimming together. I drew such strength from Freddy, as I was so out of my depth and comfort zone.

Spiritual sex

Two people playing and laughing and crying with rich passion opens a Pandora's box that has no lid or base. It funnels energy of the gods and goddesses. The depth of your heart is searched and released from all negativity. The pipeline of your beauty shines into the infinite sea of love. I used to have a male friend called Kieran. We loved each other; there was no competition, and love flowed with no jealousy. Jealousy kills love. Never let anyone (including yourself) limit your enjoyment of rich, safe, spiritual sex. It is so amazing. I dare you! You can read all the sex books; however, allow yourself to experience that divine exchange of energies.

As I write this, I am on a beach with many naked people, and the wonder of being naked is that we have nothing to hide on the outside. Yet are we truly naked? How many traumas do we carry into the act of sexual union?

Our bodies reveal so much hurt as we overeat, smoke, use drugs and alcohol, diet excessively, and practice self-abuse of all kinds.

Imagine becoming a sacred god and goddess to each other, allowing you to let go of the self you usually show to the world and reconnect with your true nature. Imagine touching foreheads and saluting with, "Namaste"... I salute from my spirit in me to the spirit in you!

Imagine that you could attract a partner who loves his or her mind, body, and spirit and has qualities that you are creating in *you*.

Imagine reading books like *The Multi-Orgasmic Couple: Sexual Secrets Every Couple Should Know* by Mantak Chia, Maneewan Chia, Douglas Abrams, and Rachel Carlton Abrams and many other creative, well-researched books that our Western culture is embracing that express ideas from the East, particularly India and China. When ideological religions suppressed open discussion on sexuality, they did a great disservice to humans loving from a place of sacred spirituality. I do believe that, if we learned to heal our fears around sexuality and connect to the divine in each of us, peace would dissolve so much pain—especially in the male.

Our sexuality is one of the most powerful, creative, blissful forces we possess, and it is also a path to spiritual enlightenment. As you journey along this path, sexuality becomes a gateway to divine bliss.

Among the most powerful sexual blocks are shame, guilt, doubt, discouragement, and embarrassment. I sometimes ask people in talks, "Do you have sexual fantasies?" Slowly people raise their hands. Then, not to embarrass anyone, I ask, "What happens to your body? Does it feel good or does it feel irritated?"

Most reply it's a good feeling. Then I ask, "How many here would love to love their own bodies the same way as the best lover they have ever had or would like to have loved their bodies? The answers come with hands raised high, nobody being shy. Then I suggest, "Well, what about you choosing to become the best lover to yourself, so you can truly inform any lover you attract?" Then we begin to hear people talk on a new level, where trust builds and hugs are given freely!

Positive sexual experiences

So often we hear what is wrong or abusive. Now I hear from people how they experience great intimacy during sex. They say they can laugh out loud; experience a sense of timelessness; love with a warm, open heart; lose their ego; feel carefree; completely let go; experience bliss, unbounded love, expansion, and connection to the divine. Most of all I hear about nonattachment to performance.

Deepak Chopra wrote:

> *In our culture "good sex" is usually defined in terms of technique and performance. We overlook that sex is a creative act, which doesn't need to be critiqued or evaluated.*

It took years for me to learn this. Sex can produce new feelings and insights. I actually got the inspiration to write this book during sex.

I am writing this as I listen to One Tribe's recording called "Earth Chant." It feels very appropriate for playing during sex with someone you want to be with and who wants to be with you.

Negative beliefs around sex

I had to clear out a lot of negative beliefs about sex before I could be a lover to myself or anyone else. These are some of the things that arose:

- Fundamental religions so often imply that sex is full of sin and that I must be separate from God to have sex! So sex and spirituality must be kept separate, and if I engage in sex, I must be secretive.
- Sex is dirty and lasts only minutes.
- I must not get a woman pregnant. (My mother's fear soon became my fear.)
- I must be in love before sex.
- I cannot ask for what I love.
- I may go to hell if I like sex.

- Kissing is dirty. (I was spanked when I was found kissing my five-year-old cousin; I was only five at the time.)
- Orgasms will take away my energy! (What a limiting belief.)
- I am too old for sex after forty. (How crazy! The best sex I have ever had I had when I was over sixty!)

Because of these negative beliefs, I kept my sexual behavior extremely secretive, which led to unhealthy behaviors.

I liked sex too much! Partners whom I attracted in early relationships told me I was obsessed with sex. So guilt and shame were always present.

I feel vulnerable admitting this, but I visited sex parlors, especially during my first marriage. One woman in New Zealand said genuinely, "You are a beautiful man. Why do you need to come here?" I was so shocked that women could find me attractive—I had a deep belief that I was ugly, especially when my college lecturer got me drunk and raped me.

I know I still have work to do on this aspect of my life. Reading *The Way of the Superior Man: A Spiritual Guide to Mastering the Challenges of Women, Work, and Sexual Desire*, by David Deida, is assisting me to dissolve many secrets that this male has carried.

Let me quote from section five, entitled "Your Dark Side":

> *To live free in spirit, you must be willing to face your fears and let go of anything that limits your love. The attachment to comfort and security is what limits most men in their capacity to make a spiritual touchdown.*

I love David Deida's quote: *"Make love as if death were imminent."* I have often said to my past partner, "I would love to die making love!" This contemplation strips away so much of my conditioning and so many of my false masks. I am completely vulnerable, naked and yet, as David Deida wrote in *Finding God Through Sex: Awakening the One of Spirit Through the Two of Flesh*:

> *…give the gift that would be the last gift of love, the giving that would leave you complete in death, nothing left ungiven …*

Make love now, as if death were imminent. Give yourself completely in love.

I'm listening to Nitin Sawhney's song, "Falling"—a brilliant tune that inspires me as I write this.

My affirmation

By the way, my Louise Hay affirmation card this morning was: *"I am my own unique self."*

Then I opened *Heart Thoughts* by Louise Hay and read the same affirmation! How's that for being "in the flow"?

Let me quote something that is apt for my heart to open a little more:

> *You are not your father. You are not your mother. You are not any of your relatives. You are not your teachers at school, nor are you the limitations of your early religious training. You are yourself… There is no competition and no comparison. You are worthy of your own love and your own self-acceptance. You are a magnificent being. You are free. Acknowledge this as the new truth for yourself. And so it is.*

Now I'm dancing to Fat Freddy's "Drop"—a fabulous tune recommended to me by my lovely son Simon, who often says: "Dad, have you heard this track?" He is such a dynamic man in the making. I love him.

I finish this chapter with a little story that may assist you in coping with any disgust or criticisms that may be in your mind!

The Monk and the Woman

> *Two Buddhist monks were journeying from one monastery to another when they came across a beautiful, but timid, young woman standing by a river bank, rather frightened to cross the swift flowing river. The elder of the two monks offered to carry*

her across, and she readily agreed. She climbed up on to his shoulders, and he waded across, leaving the woman, dry and thankful, on the other side.

The two monks continued on their way, but the younger of the two was very disappointed in the older monk's behavior. Had he forgotten that he was a monk, and that he shouldn't touch any woman, let alone a beautiful young woman? What would people say? Did he not know the rules of the order they both belonged to? And so on. The young monk's lecture lasted for a few good miles.

Finally, unable to take any more, the older monk interrupted the flow of criticism and said to his companion: "Brother, I left the girl by the riverbank. Are you still carrying her?"

I hope you can let go! I am learning—maybe always will be learning—to let go, yet with an ever-deeper sense of forgiveness of self and others.

DIVE

17

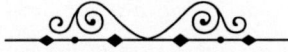

Do we accept violence as okay and sex as evil? Many shades of grey!

As Eileen Caddy, co-founder of Findhorn Eco village community in Scotland, said: *"Life is full and overflowing with the new. But it is necessary to empty out the old to make room for the new to enter."*

When I see what people are reading on the beach—*Fifty Shades of Grey* by E. L. James (in different languages)—I realize how we have separated spirituality from sex. Does this enticing story of erotic fantasies meet the *true* needs or the *warped* needs of people? Or are we so very "alienated" from loving ourselves spiritually and sexually? Do we need danger and near abuse to turn us on? Two men spoke to me today when they found out I was writing a book about *warrior* love, and healing. One of them queried with wry smiles, "Is it like *Fifty Shades of Grey?*" Do we end up requiring near violence instead of love to turn us on? This I believe rationalizes our ability to give warped, secret love.

I risk judging; yet we have more abuse surfacing today than ever before. It is strange how we trick ourselves about being able to watch hard violence of people being killed or tortured, yet we outlaw beautiful sex films! What crazy logic or poor consciousness is that? Or am I not well "domesticated"?

Many people, me included, go along letting relationships work well and give us a lot of pleasure until we suddenly reach our pleasure tolerance. This is an artificial barrier I set for myself because guilt comes in with such force. I find myself sabotaging connections with people I love or who are just friends. How crazy to separate sex and spirituality. I think there is a study that says more sexual abuse occurs in so-called "down-your-throat" religious families than in non-religious families. I am sure the Victorian era had a part to play.

To me, sex is deeply spiritual, and then the divine lets me find innocence—not the potential abuser or sinful male in me. I sense that religious doctrine has done so much harm to our love of joy, pleasure, and happiness. Guilt is such a false controller of human beings.

Wouldn't it be lovely to wake up with this short mindfulness verse from Thích Nhất Hạnh in his book *Happiness* asks:

"As you wake up in the morning and open your eyes, you may like to recite this short mindfulness verse, called a *gatha:*

> *Waking up this morning, I smile.*
> *Twenty-four brand new hours are before me.*
> *I vow to live fully in each moment*
> *And to look at all beings with compassion.*

I would add, "Including self-compassion."

I write this to the song "Grande Parade" by Professor Trance. It goes deep into the spirit and gives divine inspiration.

I have seen so many people highly frustrated in every area of their lives because guilt runs their thoughts, beliefs, and minds. Your mind is a tool. Take mental control and listen to your inner body. Let the innocence of your body release the parasites of guilt and fear. Let the orgasm of breathing love into every cell become a meditative technique.

Spirit loves and assists enlightenment

You can start by forgiving yourself for any transgressions you think you have chosen. I love this heart thought from Sondra Ray:

"My trouble was that I did not know how to use relationships for enlightenment and for healing myself. Now I know no one can hurt me but myself. I know that if I feel hurt, there is something I have not cleared. I know that if a man leaves, someone greater is coming along. I know that there is a new way to handle relationships, a way that *always* brings me peace and joy and enlightenment no matter what happens. You too, can have this resolution. You and your partner can learn to get the maximum joy and value out of your relationship, no matter how it turns out."

In connecting to what Eckhart Tolle calls the "inner body," you will find such ecstasy in all your being! As I dance, I connect to my inner body, and transformation happens similarly through loving sex. My spirit soars with the inner body feeling so connected to the divine.

A Course in Miracles says in Lesson 68, *"Love holds no grievances."* And adds: *"To hold grievance is to let the ego rule your mind."* Later:

> *"Perhaps you do not yet fully realize just what holding grievances does to your mind. It seems to split you off from your source and make you unlike him."*
> And later *"When I let all my grievances go I know I am perfectly safe."*

I love letting go grievances yet they can come back to haunt me and I have further work to do!

When religion has become an ideology, when men use and abuse scripture to have power over human beings, they inflict great pain by denying sensual pleasure through our animalistic bodies. I suggest, if you repress the energy of love, love will become abusive and addictive.

So I invite you to listen to your body and the wonderful animalistic virtues it has—like I did with Freddy the Dolphin.

However, we need to experience this inner body that is eternal. Your love, together with the divine love, is going to lift you up.

I am playing "Love Is Going To Lift You Up" by Bobby Womack.

This reminds me of "The Smuggler," a story of the obvious—yet so unseen—just like how doctors or so-called experts are not prepared to see the connection between mind, body, and soul!

The Smuggler

Every day, Mustafa took his straw-laden donkey across the border. But one day, he was stopped by a customs officer, who eyed him suspiciously.

"What have you got in that straw?" he asked. "Are you carrying any contraband goods across the border? If you are, you'll have to pay a fee."

"Look for yourself," replied Mustafa. "I'm hiding nothing!" The customs officer poked about and found nothing.

This went on, day after day. Sometimes he would look in the donkey's mouth, even under the tail! Nevertheless, the customs officer vowed he would never stop searching.

This went on for ten years, and the customs officer retired. However, the ex-officer thought one day he might have been smuggling gold dust in the donkey's fur.

One day he was walking through the market and he saw a familiar face. It was Mustafa without his donkey. "Hey you! Come here! Aren't you are the man with the donkey laden with straw?"

"Yes I am," replied Mustafa.

"And you were smuggling weren't you? I am convinced you were. I searched you every day but I couldn't find anything, because you were very crafty. But you can tell me now. Were you smuggling?"

"Yes I was!"

"I knew it! What were you smuggling?"

"Donkeys!" said Mustafa with a big smile.

What negative thoughts do we smuggle into our beautiful minds, bodies, and souls? Our bodies never lie. We, in our minds, lie to it. Then we wonder why we are full of fear and dis-ease!

My love to you!

DIVE

18

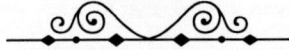

Reflection on transition

Good day! It's late afternoon and it's my 29th day here in Crete. The Cicadas raise their throbbing noise as the heat fumes down the valley like an inferno.

My Louise Hay card today: *"I am here at the right time. The work I do on myself is not a goal, it is a process. I choose to enjoy the process."*

And I add the quote from the back of *You Can Heal Your Life*: *"If we are willing to do the mental work, almost anything can be healed."*

My daughter sent me a text this morning: "Lots of Love." That meant a lot to me as I play Chloe Goodchild's evocative song: "How I Love You"!

I have just picked up Herman Hesse's book *Siddhartha*; it spoke to me deeply about my retreat. Let me quote:

> *Siddhartha reflected on his state. He found it difficult to think; he really had no desire to, but he forced himself. Now, he thought that all these transitory things have slipped away from me again; I stand once more beneath the sun, as I once stood as a small child. Nothing is mine, I know nothing, I possess nothing, I have learned nothing. How strange it is! Now, when I am no longer young, when my hair is fast growing grey, when strength begins to diminish, now I am beginning again like a child."* *He had to smile again. Yes, his destiny was strange! He was going backwards, and now he again stood empty and naked*

*and ignorant in the world. But he did not grieve about it; no,
he even felt a great desire to laugh; to laugh at himself, to laugh
at this strange foolish world!*

I feel when reading this that there is a bird in my heart that wants
to be free to sing and fly. That bird is love.

I am near... No, I am *in* a massive change and transition to my life
with the vulnerable side of me exposed. Yet somehow I feel free. I have
no idea what will happen when I return home, and yet I feel like the
frog that was hard of hearing! I love to tell this little story:

Two Frogs

*A group of frogs was traveling in unfamiliar territory when
two of them fell into a pit. The companions of the unfortunate
pair gathered round the pit and were horrified to find that it
was very deep.*

*The two frogs in the pit were jumping and jumping,
occasionally coming close to the top, but never quite making it.
At first their companions were optimistically encouraging their
efforts, but as the day wore on, and the numerous attempts at
escape were unsuccessful, they became more pessimistic.*

*"It's no use," they shouted down. "It looks as if you're going to
die. There's nothing we can do to help. Why don't you save yourselves
the effort and frustration and just resign yourselves to your fate?"*

*One of the frogs listened to the advice of the crowd up above. He
stopped attempting to jump out, and very soon was dead. However,
the other one kept on jumping; in fact, he seemed to be jumping
harder and harder, and remarkably, he eventually jumped out!*

*The other frogs congratulated him on his escape, but they
asked him, "Why did you not continue jumping? Didn't you
hear what we were saying?"*

*"Well, I saw your lips moving, but I'm deaf, so I thought
you were encouraging me the whole time," replied the frog, who
had reason to be thankful for his disability."*

Be discerning of whom you listen to!

Sometimes we listen to the crowd when we share our hurt. What we do is allow other people's pessimism or their hurt to join to ours, and we go down into the dark pit together. I often say to my clients: "Be discerning about whom you ask for advice, as you share your pain—including me. I will help you up, but I will not let you drag me down."

In change and transition there are so many people telling you that your goals are impossible (including me, if I am negative).

So I affirm that you, the reader, will think and feel carefully about the dives into my journey with openness to loving you inside! Let me remind you of the quotes at the beginning. I hope you can take them in to a deeper place in your heart:

Louise Hay: *"When I experience a problem, and we all have them, I immediately say: "Out of this situation, only good will come. This is easily resolved for the highest good of all concerned. All is well and I am safe.""*

Sondra Ray: *"One definition of love is ultimate self-approval. If you love yourself, you will automatically give others the opportunity to love you."*

Deborah Anapol: *"Love is inherently free. It cannot be bought, sold, or traded."*

David Deida: *"Giving Love-to the point of recognizing existence as love—is the purpose of your life.*

Or as Paulo Coelho puts it, *"In love lies the seed of our growth. The more we love, the closer we are to the spiritual experience."*

Don Miquel Ruiz: *"Become impeccable with your word. Don't take things personally, don't make assumptions and always do your best ... And know each time you break these agreements you can start again."*

Robert Holden adds, *"Love is about everything ... When you make love your purpose, you are fulfilling your destiny."*

Fred Lehrman states, *"The Immortal Relationship will be real for you to the extent that you can let go of two fundamental lies about your existence which you may have accepted at your birth: first, that love comes from outside of you; second, that you need love to survive. What is true is this: You are love, and nothing can kill you."*

Brene Brown: *"I now see how owning our story and loving ourselves through that process is the bravest thing that we will ever do."*

Masaru Emoto, *"Water secretly holds two energies: one of love and one of gratitude."*

The power of now

As I finish this book, I feel it is only part of what I want to share with you. I would love (even if it's a "tough" response) to hear from you about why and how you have chosen to love *you*. How do you experience your own unique *warrior* love? What has assisted you in handling jealousy in open relationships? How have your secrets of childhood abuse affected your present love life?

Have self-help groups and counseling helped you to release the past and re-parent yourself?

Has being a parent been helped by loving the true powerful person you are?

Can you say "No" to being a victim?

What is your unique journey that has made you safer to become loving, loveable and loved?

I am planning to continue writing, so if you want to send me your stories of healing love, I will include them in my next book—if you are willing. I truly want men to read other men's feelings and emotions and what has helped men love and heal, and be open and receptive to authentic change. But, that does not exclude women!

This quote by physician and psychiatrist Jerry Jampolsky sums up my feelings:

> *Giving means extending one's love with no conditions, no expectations and no boundaries. Peace of mind occurs, therefore, when we put all our attention into giving and have no desire to get anything from, or to change another person. The giving motivation leads to a sense of inner peace and joy that is unrelated to time.*

Love is letting go of fear. A great thought to meditate on.

Heart thought

Louise Hay wrote, *"I release all old hurts and forgive myself. When you hold onto the past with bitterness and anger and you don't allow yourself to experience the present moment you are wasting today."*

Here is my last contemporary story:

The Map and the Man

> *It was a particularly rainy Saturday afternoon. Two children, John and Rebecca, were becoming increasingly bored, and their father was under strict orders to keep them entertained while their mother went shopping.*
>
> *He wanted to watch the sport on television and to read his newspaper, but the children had demanded his attention. He'd tried them with paper and colored pencils, but this barely entertained them for five minutes. He'd tried the television, but they'd seen all the cartoons a dozen times. For some reason they didn't even want to play on the computer. And there were still a couple of hours before their mother returned.*
>
> *Suddenly, he had an idea. He picked up a magazine; he flicked through and found a map of the world. "Look at this,*

kids," he said. "I am going to cut this map into pieces, a bit like a jigsaw puzzle. If you can put it together again, I'll take you to McDonalds for tea! Is it a deal? ["I would prefer a different place," I can hear you say with an accompanying groan.]

The children agreed to give it a try. Their father cut up the map, gave them a pot of glue, and set them to work on the kitchen table. He meanwhile, put on the kettle, made himself a cup of coffee, and sat down with his newspaper in the living room. He was feeling very pleased with himself. "It'll take them at least an hour, he thought with a smile.

But barely ten minutes later he heard, "Finished, Dad!" He couldn't believe it. He went through into the kitchen, and there, sure enough, sitting on the table was the completed map.

"How on earth did you finish it so quickly?" He asked.

"It was easy," said John. "The map of the world was complicated, but on the other side was a picture of a man. We just put the man together."

"Yes," said Rebecca. "If you get the man right, the world takes care of itself!"

Maybe I am slightly crazy and simplistic, yet I believe we men, especially, can heal our lives by learning to love ourselves from deep respect and truth. We can make the world a safer place to live and love. We can relate to women and children with honesty, creativity, and genuine kindness. Maybe my next book will be *Everyman's Guide To Learning And Living With Love (That every woman could read!)*

As we come to the end, take a deep breath and notice how wonderful it is to be alive. Feel the connection between air and love! Just to be alive is enough. Open your heart and see everything with the eyes of love. Be full of gratitude for the life we are living so that more "good" can come in. Love being you, and the doors to love, I promise, will open in so many unexpected ways.

With your faith in the "power within" you will alchemize any deep-seated hurt. You and I will be set free to love.

Men, we *can* love and heal our lives, and make it a safer world where we can love each other and our earth. Thank you.

As John Lennon said: *"All You Need Is Love"*! It's now up to us, men and women, to find healing, truth, and courage inside the heart of love, inside ourselves. Then we will often give gratitude, appreciation, and praise.

May you live in love for the rest of your life! Be a *warrior* of truth. Then warrior love becomes a miracle for serving and healing our wounded earth. And so it is.

Bolo Hari The Blue God comes to Town by Prem Joshua is playing me out under the stars.

Thank you for reading. Do contact me at www.rogerking.info.

I give heartfelt thanks to my partner. I let her go with love. And I thank divine wisdom for this book and using me to channel it to you all.

My love and support to you all!

Roger king
August 2013, Paleochora, Crete and
December 2013, Wakefield, UK.

I affirm that the right ethical and loving publisher is coming exactly at the right time on the checker board of life, and with deep wisdom, this book will touch people's hearts for creating healing love on earth. And so it is!"

My last affirmation, as I finish my writing retreat is from Louise Hay's *Heart Thoughts*:

> *I am free. I am pure spirit and light and energy. I see myself as being free. I am free in my mind. I am free in my emotions. I am free in my relationships. I am free in my body. I feel free in my life.*

Thank you, Louise Hay.

DIVE

APPENDIX I

One-woman's story and walk to freedom from abuse by experiencing *warrior* love! Becoming brave with her truth and creating a new life.

My Miracle Within – by S Cox

The beginning

My life should have been simple, and to the outside world it was. As a 43 year old woman trapped in a little girl's mind (was that my inner child I asked myself?) only then did I realize I could be me; a caring, loving, passionate, beautiful woman that had so much to give and take; to be happy and to feel truly loved and cared for by the people I needed around me.

My story, however, wasn't so simple. The negative people in my life have caused, and still to this day cause, me pain and rejection, and the sad thing is these "Negatives" are unaware they make me feel that bad, and if they stopped to listen, rather than dwell on their own "everything is against them" lives, they would be upset and mortified for all of five minutes before their next crisis came along! To their credit, and my ultimate downfall, I had become an exceptionally good actress and liar at covering up my sickening pain; the joy of a wicked and cheeky sense of humor had become the norm at covering up any cracks that may have slightly appeared in my existence.

The big questions for me were: Why had it taken me 'til then to come to this conclusion? Was it the nervous breakdown I'd had the previous year? The little white tablets I took religiously every morning to get me through the day? My marriage breakdown after twenty-one years—and the mourning that went with that? Was it my childhood gremlins that subconsciously haunted me every day and night? Or was it just the pitiful fact that I'd let everyone walk all over me since I was a very small, dainty, fragile child?

Was I sad it had taken forty three years to admit to this? Was I resentful to the "Negatives" who had made me feel so bad about myself? Or was I scared of my future happiness? The answer, thankfully, to all of these questions was a big fat "NO!" Although I'd always known there had been problems with my life, I had been content to plod on for the sake of the people around me; whether it had been for my parents, husband, my career, or my precious children. I'd always put them first. If I had ever doubted I should not be happy with second best, then I would feel dreadfully guilty and depressed at my selfishness. After all, that was my role as a daughter, wife, mother, or employee—wasn't it?

Guilt had been, and still was, a massive issue in my life. I couldn't remember a time when I hadn't felt stomach curdling guilt about something. Guilt that overlapped the next round of guilt, which overlapped the next and so on, until I can't remember a time without guilt; an awfully vicious circle. Guilt had been my life and for good reasons. From a young child all I ever wanted was to be loved and adored by the people around me and yes, I can confess now, they had let me down.

My first childhood memory was of me stood in a kitchen, looking up and playing with the dustbin. Why I remember this, as I was only about 18 months old, I am unsure, but the sun beaming through the small window by the sink is so very vivid in my mind. Could this have been the start of my inner child before it all went wrong? The memories before this are ones my mum had put in my head, of me eating and swallowing a bar of soap, sat in my baby bath, while she and my godmother chatted on, oblivious to my mischievous antics, until they noticed bubbles coming out of my mouth when I giggled. Or when I enjoyed the cats dinner because I thought cat food tasted nice! After that, I remember living in Germany for a short time while my dad was posted there with the army. The sun was warm and I enjoyed the paddling pool in the shared garden with the other kids, and my mum buying me a go-cart in town; me sitting in it on the bus all the way home with everyone chattering in German around me. I can remember I smiled all the way back and I was so happy.

We moved from Germany soon after that, and from there I remember going in the back door of a hotel with David, my mum's "special friend" and my dad's "ex-friend". The hotel kitchen was warm, cozy and smelt of a lovely Sunday dinner. This was David's parents' hotel in Harrogate. To me it was a heaven of thick pile, expensive carpet, posh rooms that smelt of wood polish, gorgeous antique furniture, and interesting ornaments. One, my Nan still has, of a cobbler mending a shoe, sat on a stool. In those days he used to wear a pair of tiny metal glasses perched on the end of his nose, but they have since been mislaid and lost after several house moves—all of which to smaller, more practical residences as they grew older. Nan is a healthy, exciting, ninety-one year old—one of life's little gems. My dear sweet granddad passed away a number of years ago, from the cruel and very ugly disease called Cancer. These total strangers, all those years ago, instantly became my precious grandparents who in my later childhood and my adulthood, became my strength to carry on. I loved them dearly from that first visit and still do.

We soon moved into a rented terrace house that backed onto the hotel. For a tiny child of three, I loved spending time with my granddad in his workshop in the basement of their hotel, cooking with my Nan and Auntie Rhoda, their helper, and when I got in the way, or it was time to serve dinner to the residents, they used to let me count all the one pence's granddad kept in a big glass jar in the office. They were happy times. Our house had a coal fire… mum hated it and the mess that went with it. I got measles and gave them to my mum. Was this the start of me knowing she was a "Negative"?

I started nursery in Harrogate. Mum took me while David started working for an open cast mining company. I loved nursery; the milk, the snoozes on mattresses in the afternoon, and the mixing with the other children. This is where I first encountered the bullies of the world. Aged four, I was pushed into a rosebush by a boy. I can't remember the tears, but I'm sure there were lots. I can, however, remember the pain and the blood from the deep scratches on my legs, back, and hands, through my torn woolen tights. This was the start of my long journey with the "Negatives".

Three years of working on myself...

The first thing I'd like to say is: "Wow! I've survived!" I'm not sure how… it all seems a little fuzzy now; the lows, the very lows, and the "never going to come out of these lows", are slowly becoming a distant memory—and given time, a memory that will seem so unreal it never even belonged to me!

My deep feeling of relief, excitement, and normality, is overwhelming and although I'm fully aware that these feelings can dissolve much more quickly than it's taken to put them safely in my inner thoughts, I am very happy they are there, and where I definitely want them to stay (forever).

In two years, I have faced my childhood abuser, tackled my inner child gremlins, left my husband of 21 years, taken redundancy, set up a new business, got divorced, nursed a dying friend to the end, and started a new life that is mine… all mine!

Each one has been challenging; a huge challenge, if taken one at a time. If taken as a whole, over a two year period it has been a fight for survival. A fight, which at first made me very ill; to a point where I didn't want to live at all! Each of these challenges has made me stronger, made me a better person, and more honest with myself and the people close to me. One of the big questions in the beginning was: "Why do I still have these people around me when they made me feel so bad?" For family members it's harder to choose to walk away; a friend or acquaintance it's easier, but at times still difficult. I would often sit with friends and family members for hours, listening to their problems, heartbreaks, and general day to day grumbles—without even a reference or interest to me.

No more, why should I? I can now choose to make my own decisions; to spend my precious time with people I want to love, because they care and love me with a passion in return. Over time I've found people hurtful, not that they've set out to be that way, but because sometimes, they are so selfishly wrapped up in their own little worlds and self-pity, that they can't see beyond their own hidden away hurt child.

I was a hurt child, growing up an only, or as I'd like to say, lonely child, with a mother that never said she loved me… She does love me, I've no doubt, but those three words choked her. The only words that came out from her were like venom, poison, that cut me to the core every time she spoke. A father who suddenly disappeared when I was only two and a stepfather who abused me mentally, physically, and sexually, after grooming me like only a pimp would.

I embarked into married life at twenty-one. At last, I could love and be loved by someone and be a perfect wife and later a perfect mum. I'm not sure when that bubble burst really… if it was my inner child that ate away in me, the disappointment of the man I thought I'd married had changed, the pressures of being a mum, working horrendous hours and travelling the lengths of the UK… or just the fact that the "Negatives" in my life were eating away all the nice parts of me? I didn't like what I was becoming or what they were actually turning me into.

The decision to change was unbearable. The guilt, the selfishness, the "what people might say", the "what happens next?" All of which came to one answer in my head: It would be better if I wasn't here! I wouldn't have to face any of this if I was dead! I never feared death, why would I? Nothing could ever make the bad thoughts go away, the self-harming, the ways of ending it all and the eating disorder… These were the only ways I could take control of a life that had very much become not mine! Then I questioned myself: "This was definitely a coward's way out. What about my precious sons? What would they do without a mum? How would they cope with their own lives?" So basically, my children saved me and unless they ever read this, they will never know!

Gradually, through support from [proper] friends, my counselor and Soul Brother, Roger, and the love for my gorgeous sons, I have nurtured and cared for myself, given myself time to adjust, challenged myself to become the person I now love. I am a survivor, because I now want to live.

The miracle within

Learning to love the person I now am seems easy. Yes the journey I have been through has been tough. I have lived the past three years day by day, gradually enjoying the "positives" in my life; those being the precious people I have attracted, the possessions I can now afford, and the many adventures I can now relive with the wonderful memories I have.

My heart is full of happiness for having the fight in me to survive the "Negatives" in my life, that eventually crumbled my shear existence; and for winning the battle for the flame of my candle that dimed, but never went out, but is now shining brighter than ever. And the beauty of life I can enjoy with the abundance of energy I now have—life is wonderful!

Throughout my journey, I have embraced positive feelings and pushed those horrid negative thoughts to the furthest, darkest place, to lock them away hopefully forever. Yes, they will reappear I'm sure, but as each day passes I become stronger and so focused on the positives that although they may bother me, they will never fester for long.

My story doesn't end there. I have grown into a successful business woman, earning the money I've worked hard for and reaping the rewards of my determination, including a house I'd always dreamed of, a new car parked in the drive, and a lover who fulfills me. And in return, I have become a passionate woman who now loves the whole experience of love making. My sons, who have stood by my difficult decisions, with which they have sometimes felt uncomfortable, have grown to take their mum for who she now is. And I know they are very proud. My final icing on my now huge cake is, after twenty years of searching for my biological father, through all my worries and life experiences, I have found him!

I'd tried all the usual avenues: online searches, writing to dozens of people in the phone book with his surname in the area of his last known address, electoral rolls… the list became endless. During a particularly challenging working day, I felt the urge once again to search the Internet. A website caught my eye—no find no fee. What had I got to lose? I filled in the only three details I had: His name, date of birth, and last known address, and pressed "submit". By 5pm I had the news

I'd always dreamed of. The rest is history. We are back in contact after 44 years apart, I have a brother and sister I adore, and an extended family I never knew existed. My dad is a wonderful man; the father I always dreamed of through those dark nights, and one that really cares and loves me as a daughter. We don't need to dwell on the lost years; we just embrace what we've got now and the love we can give each other going forward.

Finally...

I can now look in a mirror, shop window, or glimpse my reflection, and truly say: "I love myself and who I have become" and give thanks for having the strength and determination to want to survive. It has definitely been worth the fight! I am truly blessed.

DIVE

APPENDIX II

Healing Holistic Practices I Have Tried and Found Helpful

- **Open up your arms every day wide and say with feeling:** "I am open and receptive to all good from the infinite universe of love, joy, and wisdom. All life loves and supports me. And so it is." Then give thanks.
- **Nutrition:** Eat organic and raw food. Read books like *The Gerson Therapy: The Proven Nutritional Program for Cancer and Other Illnesses* by Charlotte Gerson. What I got from this was learning to juice vegetables and fruits daily. Although the book is aimed at healing cancer, it provides so much information about colonics and much more.
- **Reflexology and massage:** Indulge in these therapeutic treatments.
- **Exercise:** Join yoga, trampoline, or Dance for Life groups. Go to the gym and get good instruction. And have fun. Cycle and walk in nature's beauty. Swim in the sea. Try windsurfing. Dance outside in the rain!
- **Mind:** Repeat positive affirmations. (I post them around so wherever I am in the house or office I see them.) Practice mirror work. Fill your iPod with books like *The Power Within* and *You Can Heal Your Life*. Play inspirational CDs in the car and play them as you travel.
- **Alternative therapies:** Search out bioenergetics and rebirthing and other forms of counseling. Join groups like Heal Your Life. Learn Tai Chi. Experiment with free dance like 5 Rhythms from Gabrielle Roth—or my version, Dance For Life (see www.

rogerking.info). Build a stream of music you love from your heart. And when you get stuck, just dance! Or roll on your bed. Let the feelings come.

- **Emotional Freedom Technique EFT** is a wonderful way of freeing yourself of emotional clutter. Do check out my EFT session with Gwyneth Moss. The session is disc 2 from the EFT Helps advanced learning and borrowing benefits DVD set with Gwyneth Moss available from www.emotional-health.co.uk
- **Spirit:** Meditate and just giving thanks daily. Sing when you get up! Make up positive songs in the shower.
- **Expand your knowledge:** Read books that are highly inspiring. Check out Dr. Wayne Dyer, Deepak Chopra, Louise Hay, Sondra Ray, Don Miguel Ruiz, Nena and George O'Neil, Marianne Williamson, and Robert Holden. One of my favorites is a special little book called *The Door of Everything* by Ruby Nelson. Read children's stories like *The Little Prince* and magical stories from spiritual masters.

Note: You can always see when a book is truly read and not sitting on the shelves. I mark mine and turn pages and highlight. I write down quotes, especially if they speak to me. Books usually choose me, based upon what I need to learn next. Robert Holden's *Lovability: Knowing How to Love And Be Loved* is such an authentic dream of new possibilities. Another book that stirred my soul is *Mutant Message Down Under: A Woman's Journey into Dreamtime Australia* by Marlo Morgan. It maybe fiction however, it will blow your mind, body, and spirit to a place of infinite possibilities.

I once gave a man who was begging at the roadside a copy of *The Power of Your Subconscious Mind* by Joseph Murphy. He was delighted. Just be willing to learn; then teach those who want to learn. Then life becomes so much more fun and wonderful.

Dedications

Antoine De Saint-Exupery, *The Little Prince.* (Wordsworth Editions1995), 93.

Bill Darlison, *The Shortest Distance* (Diggory Press 2006 Spiritual Stories re-told. Permission)

Introduction

Louise L. Hay, *LIFE Reflections on Your Journey.* (Hay House 1995), 142.

Sondra Ray, *Loving Relationships.* (Celestial Arts 1980), 20.

Dr Deborah Anapol, *The Seven Natural Laws of Love.* (Elite Books 2005), 12.

Paulo Coelho, *Quote of The day.* July 30 1998

David Deida, *Finding God Through Sex Awakening the One of Spirit Through the Two of Flesh* (Sounds True Inc 2005), 278.

Don Miquel Ruiz, *The Four Agreements. A Practical Guide to Personal freedom* (Amber-Allen Audio Publishing produced by Janet mills Read By Peter Coyote.)

Robert Holden, *Loveability. Knowing How To Be Loved.* (Hay House. E Kindle)

Fred Lehrman, *Immortal Relationships Loving Relationships* Sondra Ray Celestial Arts.1980), 136.

Brene Brown, *The Gift Of Imperfection.* (Hazelden 2010), iv.

Masaru Emoto, *Messages from Water and the Universe.* (Hay House 2010), 20.

Sondra Ray, *Loving Relationships.* (Celestial Arts 1980), 74-5.

M. Gandhi, *My life is a message, Life of Gandhi* (1968) chap13 reel 31

Dr Deborah Anapol, *The Seven Natural Laws of Love.* (Elite Books 2005), 96.

Sondra Ray, Loving Relationships. (Kyle Os Chap The Secrets,) 75.

Dive 1

Dr Wayne W.Dyer, *The Shift Taking Your Life from Ambition to Meaning.* (Hay House.2010), 82.

Dr Wayne W Dyer. *The Power of Intention.* (Hay House.2004), 4.

Brene Brown, *The Gift of Imperfection.* Hazeldene.2010

TED is a global set of conferences owned by the private non-profit Sapling Foundation, under the slogan "ideas worth spreading".

Dive 2

Louise L. Hay, *Wisdom Cards A 64-card Deck* (Ilustrated by Eris Klien & Sarajo Freden Hay House 2000).

Louise L. Hay, *You Can Heal Your Life.* (Hay House, 2009), 14.

Dr Deborah Anapol, *The Seven Natural Laws of Love.* (Elite Books, 2005), 11.

Dr Deborah Anapol, *The Seven Natural Laws of Love.* (Elite Books, 2005), 27.

Dr Wayne W.Dyer, *The Shift Taking Your Life from Ambition to Meaning.* (Hay House.2010), 91.

Louise L Hay, *The Power is Within You.* (Hay House, 2009), 137.

Susan Hayward, *A Guide for the Advanced Soul.* (In tune books Australia 1984)

Eric Butterworth, *Discover the Power Within You: A Guide to the Unexplored Depths Within. (Harper Collins 1989).*

Louise L. Hay, *You Can Heal Your Life.* (Hay House, 2009), 1.

Lynne Forrest and Eileen Meagher, *Guiding Principles for Life Beyond Victim Consciousness* (Conscious Living Media 2011)

Sondra Ray, *Loving Relationships.* (Celestial Arts 1980), 128.

Dive 3

Peter J. Benson, *The Polyamory Handbook A Users Guide* (AuthorHouse 2008) E Kindle 1.01

Dr Deborah Anapol, *The Seven Natural Laws of Love.* (Elite Books, 2005), 79-78

Peter J. Benson, *The Polyamory Handbook A Users Guide* (AuthorHouse 2008) E Kindle 1.01 1.02

Dr Deborah Anapol, *The Seven Natural Laws of Love.* (Elite Books, 2005), 5,11,27,45,61,77,93.

Kahil Gibran, *The Prophet* (William Heinmen 1980), 83-86.

David Deida, *Finding God Through Sex.* (Sounds True Inc 2005), 261.

Dive 4

Sondra Ray, *Loving Relationships.* (Celestial Arts 1980), 71.

Dive 5

Robert Holden**,** *Loveability. Knowing How To Be Loved.* **(**Hay House.) E Kindle, 6

John Bradshaw, *Home Coming Reclaiming & championing your inner child* (Judy Piatkus 1999), 65.

John K. Pollard III, *Self Parenting The Complete Guide to Your Inner Conversations.*

Dive 6

Louise L. Hay, Heart Thoughts A Daily Guide To Finding Inner Wisdom (Hay House India 1990), 120.

Dive 7

Sondra Ray**,** *Loving Relationships* (Celestial Arts 1980 Quote from A Course In Miracles), 62.

Don Miquel Ruiz**,** *The Four Agreements* (Amber-Allen Audio Publishing produced by Janet mills Read By Peter Coyote.)

Dr Wayne W. Dyer, *Inspiration Your Ultimate Calling* (Hay House 2006), 119.

Dr Wayne W.Dyer *The Shift: Taking Your Life from Ambition to Meaning* (Hay House 2010), 64.

Dive 8

Anthony de Mello, *Song of The Bird* (Doubleday New York 1990)

Dr Wayne W.Dyer *The Shift: Taking Your Life from Ambition to Meaning* (Hay House 2010), 92. Rumi *Treasury of Spiritual Wisdom*

Dive 9

Louise L. Hay, *Wisdom Cards A 64-card Deck* (Ilustrated by Eris Klien
& Sarajo Freden Hay House 2000).

Susan Hayward, *A Guide for the Advanced Soul.* (In tune books Australia
1984) Quote Vernon Edwards.

Anthony de Mello, *Song of The Bird* (Doubleday New York 1990)

Nancy Kline, *Time To Think Listening to ignite the Human Mind* (Ward
Lock Octopus Group 1999)

Dive 10

David Deida, *Finding God Through Sex.* (Sounds True Inc 2005), 171-2

Susan Hayward, *A Guide for the Advanced Soul.* (In tune books Australia 1984)
Quote Eileen Caddy

David J. Wolpe's book, *Teaching Your Children About God: A Modern
Jewish Approach.* (Henry Holt 1996)

Dive 11

Louise L. Hay, *Wisdom Cards A 64-card Deck* (Ilustrated by Eris Klien
& Sarajo Freden Hay House 2000).

Don Miquel Ruiz, *The Mastery of Love. A practical Guide to the Art of
Relationships* (Amber-Allen Audio Publishing produced by Janet
mills read by Jill Eikenberry & Michael Tucker.)

Susan Hayward, *A Guide for the Advanced Soul.* (In tune books
Australia 1984)

Quote Eileen Caddy

Dive 12

Louise L. Hay, *Wisdom Cards A 64-card Deck* (Ilustrated by Eris Klien
& Sarajo Freden Hay House 2000).

Deepak Chopra *The Path To Love Spiritual lessons for creating the love
you need* (Random House 2000), 170.

Robert Holden. *Loveability. Knowing How To Be Loved.* (Hay House. E Kindle

Forgiveness undoes the blocks Chap 5)

Dr Deborah Anapol, *Polyamory in the 21st Century: Love Intimacy & Multiple Partners* (Rowman & Littlefield 2010), 121.

DIVE 14

Joeseph Allen Boone, *Kinship with all of life* (Harper Collins 1976)

Dive 15

Greg Bradon, *The Divine Matrix Bridging Time, Space, Miracles, and Belief* (Hay House 2007)

Gabrielle Roth, *Sweat Your Prayers, Movement as Spiritual Practice* (Penguin Putnam 1998)

Sondra Ray, *Loving Relationships.* (Celestial Arts 1980), 74-75.

Sondra Ray, *Loving Relationships.* (Celestial Arts 1980), 56-7.

Dr Wayne Dyer. *The Power of Intention. Change the Way You Look at Things and the Things You Look at Change* (Hay House. 2004) Front cover

Dive 16

Michelle Pauli, *Spiritual Sex* (MQ Publications 2002),14.

Deepak Chopra The Path To Love. *Spiritual lessons for creating the love you need* (Random House 2000), 149.

David Deida, *The Way of the Superior A Spiritual Guide to Mastering the Challenge of Women, Work, and Sexual Desire* (Sounds True inc 2004), 127

David Deida, *Finding God Through Sex Awakening the One of Spirit Through the Two of Flesh* (Sounds True Inc 2005), 278. 282

Louise L. Hay, *Wisdom Cards A 64-card Deck* (Ilustrated by Eris Klien & Sarajo Freden Hay House 2000).

Louise L. Hay, Heart Thoughts A Daily Guide To Finding Inner Wisdom (Hay House India 1990), 219.

Dive 17

Susan Hayward, *A Guide for the Advanced Soul.* (In tune books Australia 1984)

Quote Eileen Caddy

Thich Nhat Hanh. *Happiness. Essential Mindfulness Practices* (Parallax Press publishing division of the United Buddhist Church. 2009), 18.

Sondra Ray, *Loving Relationships.* (Celestial Arts 1980), 74.

Foundation For Inner Peace *A Course In Miracles.* (1985), 114 Lesson 68.

Dive 18

Louise L. Hay, *Wisdom Cards A 64-card Deck* (Ilustrated by Eris Klien & Sarajo Freden Hay House 2000

Louise L. Hay, *You Can Heal Your Life.* (Hay House, 2009), Back cover

Hermann Hesse. *Siddhartha* (Peter Owen Ltd. & Pan Books1954), 75.

Jerry Jampolsky *Love is Letting Go Of Fear,* (Celestial Arts 1979),

Louise L. Hay, Heart Thoughts A Daily Guide To Finding Inner Wisdom (Hay House India 1990), 93.

Songs: In order.

Cliff & Nash, "I can see clearly now"

Bill Withers, "Lean on Me" Album *Still Me*

Cat Stevens, "Moonshadow"

Carmel McCreagh "We Love Love"

Donna De Lory "Bathe in these waters.

Bobby Womak "Love Is Gonna Lift You Up" Album The Bravest man in the Universe.

Chiwoniso Listen to the Breeze" Album Superclub Presents Nomads 7

All stories came from (which were retold and annotated) Bill Darlison's *The Shortest Distance—101 stories from the world's spiritual traditions.*

- *The Snake in the Cup*, 270 words
- *The King and the Beggar's Gift*, 325 words
- *The Stag at the Pool*, 191 words
- *A Sufi Story*, 251 words
- *Starfish on the Beach*, 143 words
- *Hiding the Secret*, 276 words
- *Stones or Bread*, 256 words
- *The Doctor's Diagnosis*—A Sufi Tale, 166 words
- *The Sailor and the Teacher*, 235 words
- *The Mouse and the Bull*, 136 words
- Leo Buscaglia's story, *Educated Insolence: Living Loving & Learning*), 262 words (Holt, Rinehart and Winston; Book Club Edition January 1, 1982)
- *Apple Pie and Ice Cream*, 202 words Anthony de Mello (see citation)
- *The Rose and the Oak Tree*, 185 words
- *The Cat and the Coins*, 240 words
- *The Contented Fisherman*, 198 words
- *Using All Your Strength*, 163 words Henry Holt/Harper Collins 1996
- *Heaven and Hell*, 223 words
- *Feeding the Wolf*, 97 words
- *The Wolf and the Dog*, 286 words
- *The Cracked Pot*, 431 words
- *The Monk and the Woman*, 178 words
- *The Smuggler*, 217 words A Sufi story from the Middle East.
- *Two Frogs*, 227 words
- *The Map and the Man*, 245 words

Further Reading:

Nancy Kline, *More Time To Think A way of Being in the World* (Fisher King 2009)

Mantak Chia Douglas Abrams Arava, *The Multi Orgasmic Man Sexual Secrets Every man Should Know* (Thorsons 2001)

Pam Grout *E-squared Nine do-it-yourself energy experiments that prove your thoughts create your reality* (Hay House 2013)

Dr Patricia J Crane, *Ordering from the Cosmic Kitchen, The Essential Guide to Powerful Affirmations* (Crane's Nest 2002)

Gabrielle Roth *Sweat Your Prayers Movement as Spiritual Practice* (Newleaf 1997)

Florence Scovel – Shinn, *The Game of life & How to Plat It. Winning Rules for Success & Happiness* Random House Vermillion 2005)

Richard Gentle, *More Than You Think Compendium*
Quantum Mass Superstructures – Creating the World we Experience and How we Perform Miracles
(www. Lulu.com/richardgentle (2012)

Erich Fromm *The Art of Loving* (George Allen & Unwin Paperbacks 1957)

Tony Buzan, *The Power of Spiritual Intelligence 10 Ways to Tap into Your Spiritual Genius* (Thorsons 2001)

Dan Millman, *Sacred Journey of the Peaceful Warrior* (Hj Kramer inc 1991)

Joan Anderson, *A Year By The Sea, Thoughts of an Unfinished Woman* (Pan Books 2001)

Echart Tolle, *A New Earth Awakening to Your Life's Purpose* (Penguin Books 2005) & *The Power of NOW A Guide To Spiritual Enlightenment* (Hodder and Stoughton 1999)

Valarie and Paul Lynch, *Emotional healing in minutes, simple acupressure techniques for your emotions.*(Thorsons 2001)

Ken Carey, *The Third Millenium Living in the Posthistoric World* (HarperOne 1991)

Dalai Lama, *365 Daily Advice from the Heart* (Harper Collins2003)

Lightning Source UK Ltd.
Milton Keynes UK
UKOW04f2350070214

226121UK00002B/66/P